PRAISE FOR JOE NATOLI

"**A very practical guide** to success in business."

DR. DON NORMAN

DIRECTOR OF THE DESIGNLAB, UC SAN DIEGO
NIELSEN NORMAN GROUP
BESTSELLING AUTHOR OF *THE DESIGN OF EVERYDAY THINGS*

. . . . , ...

"**For designers and developers working on any interactive project, understanding strategy and user experience is an increasingly necessary skill**. Joe Natoli's *Think First* demystifies these foundational ideas and, like any good user experience, is written in a very conversational, easy to read style. Highly recommended!"

ILISE BENUN

FOUNDER OF MARKETING-MENTOR.COM
AUTHOR OF 7+ BOOKS

. . . .

"*Think First* is a practical guide to UX that **makes sense of strategy and structure**. Highly recommended!"

PETER MORVILLE

PRESIDENT, SEMANTIC STUDIOS
AUTHOR OF *INTERTWINGLED: INFORMATION CHANGES EVERYTHING*

"**Nailed it!** In the vein of *Rework* by Jason Fried, *Think First* is an insightful, iconoclastic handbook. It unrelentingly strips down aspects of software design to the brass tacks. Joe must possess some magical nutri-design juicer which he's used to extract the nutrients of dozens and dozens of textbooks, websites, references and experience and is providing it to us in a single, filled-to-the-rim shot glass of realistic scenarios, approaches and tools.

Too often we focus on the user interface design or technology aspects, but in this book Joe pulls us by the ear and points our noses at 'can you articulate the goal, and *what is its value*?' Tape the pages of this book to your wall as a daily reminder."

JONATHAN COOK

ASSISTANT VICE PRESIDENT OF ENTERPRISE
INFORMATION TECHNOLOGY & ARCHITECTURE,
NATIONAL COMMITTEE FOR QUALITY ASSURANCE (NCQA)

. . . .

"**Joe fundamentally changed the way we approach design**. With a new focus on the underlying design principles, we are able to make decisions grounded in fact, not opinions. We now understand the subtle changes that transform a good design into a *great* design. The practices we now employ are improving every step of our development practice; from prototype to final product.

Joe's influence is evident in all of our work."

PATRICK TOOHEY

SENIOR SOFTWARE ENGINEER, METTLER-TOLEDO

"**Joe has always been a step ahead of me, offering expert advice and producing results that one can only *hope* for**. He has always been the consummate professional — 5-stars, in every way, every form, every month. Joe is a hard-working problem solver of the first order, and I'd give him a 5-star recommendation to *anyone*, anytime."

MARYELLEN MOONEY

CREATIVE PROMOTIONS DIRECTOR, BON APPÉTIT MAGAZINE

. . . .

"**Joe effectively and uniquely brings the two worlds of IT and Design (sometimes at odds) together** in order to develop a product or system that works for both the business *and* the customer. Joe is intelligent, insightful, innovative and extremely talented. His experience and reputation precede him.

Expect *results*."

MIKE MATTHEWS

CREATIVE DIRECTOR, BROADRIDGE

. . . .

"**What you've put together is pure excellence**. I'm new to UX Design and have already learned essential advice, principles and methods that I can apply to our product. I hope to share this new knowledge with my team in hopes to get our product and features to the high quality we've been reaching for."

RYAN SAMSON

STUDENT, *UXD FUNDAMENTALS* COURSE

"**Incredible**. Joe's class is really impressive and really helps me reflect [on improving] my work. I feel like I'm learning more in this course than in *all* the time I spent in college!"

PAOLO ORIONE

STUDENT, *UXD FUNDAMENTALS* COURSE

. . . .

"**Greatest UX course I have ever taken**. Joe's numerous real-world examples provide an in-depth understanding of UX. Whether you're a developer or designer, this course will show you what UX *really* is."

CATHY FANG

STUDENT, *UXD FUNDAMENTALS* COURSE

. . . .

"**Great knowledge and insight!** Joe walks you through the course with ease, playfulness, humor, and great insight. With conversation-like ease, Joe exposes insights that you may have never thought of, reasoning behind each, and clear solutions. This course has so many transferable qualities; you will benefit, regardless of the type of design your career path follows."

CHITA HUNTER

STUDENT, *UXD FUNDAMENTALS* COURSE

"**I found that my knowledge of user experience design didn't even *scratch the surface* of what Joe covers**. I now realize the importance and necessity of knowing and understanding each element of User Experience — and how each element is essential to the overall quality and success of your site or app.

This is thorough training that you will only get from someone that has years of experience. I guarantee you will *never* look at user experience design the same."

CAROL

STUDENT, *UXD FUNDAMENTALS* COURSE

. . . .

"**Mr. Fred Rogers said in an interview 'The best teacher in the world is somebody who loves what he or she does and just loves it in front of you.'** Going through this course, I was reminded of this phrase over and over again. Joe clearly loves what he does, and he inspired me to love UX too! The course material is extremely well thought out, and it is delivered with a contagious joy. Wonderful experience."

PETER DAMOC

STUDENT, *UXD FUNDAMENTALS* COURSE

Photography by Jarred Sleeth.

ISBN 978-0-9863448-0-0

Published in Baltimore, Maryland, USA by Twofold LLC.
Give Good UX is a registered trademark of Twofold LLC.

Twofold/Give Good UX titles may be purchased in bulk for
educational, business, fund-raising, or sales promotional use.

For more information, please email **books@givegoodux.com**.

THINK FIRST

MY NO-NONSENSE APPROACH TO CREATING
SUCCESSFUL PRODUCTS, POWERFUL USER
EXPERIENCES + <u>VERY</u> HAPPY CUSTOMERS

JOE NATOLI

UX CONSULTANT TO THE FORTUNE 100

DEDICATION

for Eli, who has *always* believed.

SPECIAL THANKS

This is often said, but bears repeating here because it's true: this book would absolutely, positively *not* have been possible were it not for the following people.

My wife Eli, for the question that started it all: "why don't you write a book?" Your seemingly endless supply of patience, support, encouragement and clear-eyed advice is nothing short of astonishing. To have you as a partner in every aspect of life is more than I could ever dare to hope for; I love you more than I can ever possibly explain.

My children, Julianna, Sabah and Sophia, who continue to teach me some of life's most challenging, most enduring and definitely most *valuable* lessons. I love you all very, *very* much.

Brad Kell, for countless hours of editing and proofreading, always pushing me to make things clearer, crisper and simpler. I am forever grateful for your herculean effort and your friendship.

Joe and Eva Barsin, along with **Gerry and Aimee Bracken,** who have always been the first in line to get behind anything I'm doing. Your support, your encouragement and most of all your friendship mean the world to me.

Mike Matthews, for picking me up more times than I care to admit and insisting the way forward was possible. For always making yourself available over the last 20+ years, to offer guidance and wisdom, and sometimes just a friendly ear. You have given me much more than I can ever repay, and I am deeply honored to call you friend.

David Flynn, for showing the ropes to a young punk fresh out of design school with a degree of patience, kindness and respect that made all the difference — and still does. I will never forget.

Katie Kennedy for lighting a raging fire inside me for design on my *very first day* of college at Kent State University. That flame is the source of everything I have ever done, and its value is immeasurable. You taught me by example the passion necessary to keep it burning, and I am ever grateful.

John Buchanan and J. Charles Walker for firmly (and sometimes *forcibly*) instilling the conviction that great design is a whole lot more than what something looks like. Your approach, insight and guidance so many years ago continues to light the way in all that I do.

To the following people who, either directly or indirectly, took the time to share their knowledge, insights and advice with me. Your kindness, generosity and your incredible, inspiring work provided valuable lessons that last to this day:

Ilise Benun

David Collins

Art Chantry

Ken Davis

Sam Faccioben

Jason Fried

Seth Godin

Ed Gold

Kim Goodwin

Lee Goske

Whitney Hess

Michael Hyatt

Guy Kawasaki

Katie Kennedy

Karen Kennedy

Teresa Kiplinger

Steve Krug

Clement Mok

Peter Morville

Dr. Don Norman

Paul Potter

Paul Sahre

Bryan Scheer

Nathan Shedroff

Matt Simpson

David Stallsmith

Kathleen Thompson

Joe Wagner

Eliot Wagonheim

Dr. Susan Weinschenk

Sam Zappas

I owe a great debt of gratitude to my parents, Richard and Donna Natoli. You instilled a belief in me that anything was possible with perseverance and led by example. I love you both.

Finally, to all the incredible people in all of the organizations I've worked with for two and a half decades: I have learned as much from you as you hopefully did from me.

It has been, and continues to be, my *honor* to work alongside you to help realize your dreams and goals.

ABOUT THE AUTHOR

For 26 years, I have helped Fortune 100, 500 and Government organizations design and reimagine digital products to improve User Experience (UX). From strategy to features to functionality to User Interface (UI) design, I work alongside product design and development teams to help them find and remove UX-related obstacles. Which, quite conveniently, helps these organizations save or make money.

In addition, I coach and train designers and developers to deliver better experiences via online courses. I am honored to have helped more than **27,000 students** to date start a career in UX or transition from a related discipline.

Everything I have ever done has revolved around a core principle: if you're in the business of creating digital products, **those products serve as your ambassadors.**

As such, user trust and customer loyalty depend wholly on the **experience** people have with those ambassadors. If the product is hard to use, people assume it's hard to do business with you. If the site sucks, *you suck*. If the system is slow and unresponsive, *so are you*. If the app is confusing and frustrating, they're frustrated with *you too*.

Products are used by *people*, after all, so putting people and their experiences first is a pretty good place to start.

At the same time, **creation always entails cost**: time, effort, money. And every creator is looking for a way to cover that cost, along with a little extra. In order to do that, you need to design and deliver **superior product experiences** — consistently, repeatedly, over time.

In order to do *that*, you need to uncover the sweet spots between **what users expect** from the product and what the **business needs** to accomplish in order to survive and prosper.

These are strategic concerns, not tactical ones. In these scenarios the greatest tool any consultant, manager, designer or developer has is what's between his or her ears.

The *thinking* part of design and UX is the most valuable part. That's what this book is about. That's what creates the **value loop** I talk about so often, where value goes out to users, and in doing so comes back to the business as well.

There are no shortcuts to great experiences. There is only the discipline to investigate, the patience to analyze, the willingness to be wrong and a mind open enough (and *brave* enough) to admit it. *Think First* is my roadmap for practicing and applying that philosophy.

What's Your Problem?

HIGH OR LOW? TREND!

DOES NECESSARY LEVEL OF
HANDHOLDING/SUPERVISION LINE UP
W/ PROCESS/TIME BEAN?

HAS TO BE
COMMUNICATED

# OF PROSPECTS		AGENT PROCESS ⟶ T...
	6 MOS.	SELL WHAT C...
	6-18 MOS.	SELL WHAT B... CLIENTS' NEG...
	2-3 YRS.	MARKET + S...
	3-5 YRS.	BUILD A BU...

CONSUMERS	GEN X + Y: ⅓ OF U.S. P...
	BOOMERS: ¼ OF U.S. P...

MRA

INDUSTRY STUDY — 50%.
GEN X/Y-HEADED HOUSEHOLDS
NOT HAVE LIFE INSURANCE

* RESEARCH + QUA...
DON'T PURCHASE

GET BACKGROUND
↓
INCREASE KNOWLEDGE
↓

...AL MEDIA LINKING STRATEGY

YOUTUBE

...CEBOOK   TWITTER   SLIDESHARE *

The start of any project is where the greatest risk lives. Essentially, you're starting from the darkest depths of the ocean. And we're not talking about the ocean *floor* — no, you're down in one of those caverns where the only life consists of those weird creatures that glow. And it is a long, *long* way to the surface.

If this sounds like a big task, that's because it most certainly is. But if you look at all the individual parts of any design process, and if you understand how they affect each other, it becomes a lot easier to tackle. And if you devote significant time and attention to the very first order of business — your **strategy** — the foundation you build will be strong enough to withstand any weather as you move into design and coding.

Anything that was ever worth doing started with a strategy. An inspiration, a motivation, a goal. If you have a strategy, that means you know what you're doing, who you're doing it for and why it matters — both to you and the people you expect to use the end result. It means you have a solid understanding of:

(a) what *users* expect to accomplish
with what you're building, and

(b) what *you* expect to accomplish with it.

Both of these things will inform every single decision that must be made going forward. Every feature, every function, every label, every interaction and every single element that winds up on the screen will be a direct result of these two interrelated goals. So every project should start with strategy, and strategy starts with asking a very simple question:

Why Are We Doing This?

I realize that question may seem painfully obvious to you.

After all, why would anyone commit massive amounts of time, energy, resources and money to something without considering the reason for doing any of it? Or at least stopping to make sure it was the *right* reason?

Well, I don't know the answer to those questions.

But I *will* tell you that I have twenty-six years and hundreds of instances where a whole lot of blood, sweat and (mostly) tears were shed without anyone stopping to consider **why**. Without anyone stopping to look before they leapt. Without anyone stopping to **think**.

Now you're obviously pretty sharp, having picked up this book, so I doubt that I need to tell you how those ventures turned out.

Here's something you absolutely must remember: **If you fail to think first, then you fail, period**. If you fail to consider the almighty *why* with adequate effort, depth or rigor, you will miss something. And that something will sneak up and break you later. It will be expensive, and it will *hurt*.

When a product fails — from industrial products to websites, systems and apps — the reason is almost *never* technology. And to be honest with you, it's not always user experience either.

What really causes most things to fail is because nobody asked, or spent enough time validating the answer to, the question on the preceding page:

Why are we doing this?

SURFACE	VISUAL DESIGN (UI)		CONCRETE
SKELETON	INTERFACE DESIGN	NAVIGATION DESIGN	
STRUCTURE	INTERACTION DESIGN	INFORMATION ARCHITECTURE	
SCOPE	FUNCTIONAL SPECIFICATIONS	CONTENT REQUIREMENTS	
STRATEGY	BUSINESS GOALS / USER NEEDS		ABSTRACT
	← TASKS →	← INFORMATION →	

A Quick Primer: The Elements of User Experience

Back in 2002, a very wise man by the name of Jesse James Garrett wrote a book called *The Elements of User Experience*. Jesse, in the opinion of most, was the first person to accurately describe and give a name to what we now know to be UX. He's the Alan Freed* of technology, as far as I'm concerned.

Jesse's book is widely regarded as *the* big-picture book on the subject, and with very good reason. It's clear, concise and easily understandable. It also goes a long way in deconstructing UX as a practice. So we're going to start there.

The Five Planes of User Experience

The central tenet of *The Elements of User Experience* is that there are five "planes" of UX, five parts of making sure that no aspect of someone's experience with a digital product happens without explicit intent.

That means you've taken into account every possibility in terms of the intended user's motivations, expectations, environment and possible actions. You've researched, tested and analyzed to figure out what they want, what they need and what they'll be willing to *use*.

What's more, you're making **informed decisions** at every step of the design process that significantly impact what you do in the next step. And you're working in a way where you are acutely aware of how decisions at any given point in the process affect the options you may or may not have in other areas. Not the least of which are the end product's quality, feasibility and viability.

* *Radio DJ who coined the term "Rock & Roll" in 1945.*

The first plane, the place you start (and the subject of this book) is the **Strategy** plane. UX starts with the product's reason for existing in the first place. Why you created it, who it's for and what it's supposed to accomplish — for both user and creator.

The second plane is **Scope**, and it contains the features and the functions that make up the product itself.

Next up is **Structure**, which is essentially the number of places that you can go, organized by context of use. What is the person there to achieve? What are they trying to do? What are the possible paths they could take? How many do they *expect*?

Move up a level and you have the **Skeleton** plane. Here we have an optimized organization and arrangement of all the elements that make up what happens on the screen. Navigation elements, content, controls. Things you can read, things you can act on. The skeleton plane is the place where we figure out how all those things work together — not just on a single screen, but across the entire system of screens.

Finally, we get to the **Surface**, which is essentially the part that the user sees. Now we have a visual representation of everything within our reach, and visible ways to interact with what we see. At this level graphics, images and visual cues work together to deliver content and enable interactivity.

The Elements are Intimately Interrelated.

The five planes build upon each other, from a strategic point where we start thinking about the *what, why* and *who*, all the way up to the surface of the screen, where we've built something people can actually see and interact with.

Each plane is split down the middle into two very distinct categories, as shown in the diagram on page 5. These categories reflect the nature of web-based sites, software and applications, and digital product technology as a whole.

On one hand, you have **task-oriented concerns**: technology platforms, data, programming languages, logic and an interface that enables people to do things. On this side of the fence we want to know what people expect to be able to do with our product. We're interested in how will they accomplish task A, B or C:

⇒ How do they move through information?

⇒ How do they get to the things that they need?

⇒ What are they ways in which they can read, write or otherwise manipulate data?

On the other side of the split are **information-oriented concerns**:

⇒ What information is being served up, and what makes it relevant or valuable or useful?

⇒ How much data or content exists, and how is it organized and prioritized?

⇒ How is it labeled, and do those labels make sense to users?

⇒ What does it mean to the people who use it?

Good UX deals with both aspects, makes sure concerns on both sides are addressed. And when it doesn't, *things fall apart.*

The UX designer's job is not only to address information concerns and the related needs of users — it's also to insist on being very **selective** and **analytical** in designing task flows and functional elements that serve a greater goal.

And that greater goal is what I call the **value loop**: creating something that delivers value to users, so that value also comes back to the product's creator in the form of increased use, efficiency or good old fashioned dollars and cents.

Strategy Means Putting People *First*

Products are used by people, so putting users and their **needs** first is a pretty good place to start:

➡ What do they need to be able to do, and why do these things matter to them?

➡ What do they want from us, and how is that related to other goals they may have?

➡ How does using our product fit with other products they may be using?

➡ What do they expect, based on their experiences with similar (or even dissimilar) products?

These are all user-focused areas of inquiry.

People live on the other side of the fence as well, except they're funding the project. Which dictates that they're concerned with **business objectives.** Creation always entails cost — time, effort, money. And nearly every creator is looking for a way to *cover* that cost, along with a little extra.

Even if you build apps for free, there is *something* you expect to get in return. That doesn't have to be money; it could be recognition or widespread adoption. It may simply be something that you truly feel good about because it helps people who are less fortunate. Whatever the case, there are objectives you have that need to be met, measures of success that *matter*.

If the business end of the equation is actually a business, then the objective, at the end of the day, is either making money or saving money. There are one or more strategic objectives that have to be met as a result of building this thing and putting it out there into the world.

If you're responsible for helping make a product reality, then you're also responsible for uncovering **what those objectives are** and **why they matter**.

Strategy, then, is all about finding the **sweet spots** between what users want to make their lives easier and what the business needs to accomplish in order to survive, to prosper. It's about recognizing the gaps and the overlaps between those goals and thinking about how design can best serve both of these masters.

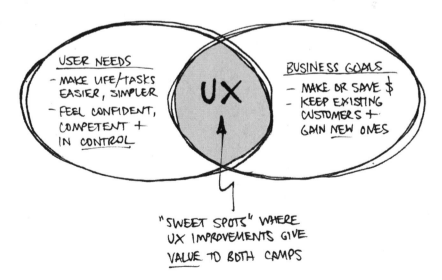

Why the Strategy Plane Rules Them All

Again: the strategy plane is the origin of the **value loop**, the part that you absolutely, positively have to get right if you want the finished product to be around longer than ten minutes.

The strategy plane is where you *think first*: where you work to uncover and qualify user needs, where you ensure that you understand all relevant business objectives. It's where you begin planting seeds of product success — or failure.

Correctly identify and address these needs and objectives, and you deliver an experience that is the answer to someone's prayer. Guess wrong, or don't do enough digging, and you identify the *wrong* needs and objectives. Which turns the product into everyone's worst nightmare, including *yours*.

When it comes right down to it, design of any kind really means problem solving. Here's some advice given to me by a colleague many years ago that couldn't possibly be more true:

If you're a designer — experienced or fresh out of school — I want you to understand that **you will not find inspiration looking at the work of other designers**.

Let that sink in a minute.

I say again: you will *not* find inspiration. What you *will* find is someone else's solution to *someone else's problem*.

You're looking at the end result, not the process. And the **process**, my friends, is where the power of design really lies. The first thing you have to do, no matter what you're creating, is identify the problem — and then make sure it's actually the *right* problem to solve.

When I was in college, my professors drilled the following fact into our heads, over and over across our four years together:

If you don't come up with a good *solution* to something, it's likely that you don't have a very good *problem*.

That's a roundabout way of saying that the key to successful design is identifying the **right problems** to solve. User experience design essentially explores feasible solutions to strategic design problems:

⇒ What matters *most*?

⇒ What issues have the most impact, the most measurable value?

⇒ What can we do to address these issues, and do we have the time, money and personnel to take that action?

⇒ Is it realistic that we can provide a solution to this particular, precise, complex problem?

Anything involving human beings is inherently messy. We're interesting creatures. What we say doesn't always match what we do, and in general we can be very difficult to please. So any problems that involve our using something are typically difficult to solve.

And if they aren't, raise the red flag — because that's a sure sign you're on the wrong path.

Innovation is a Balancing Act

Innovation occurs when tough problems are solved. For designers and developers, problem solving means uncovering the sweet spots mentioned on the previous pages. These are the places where you can do something that's unique, that's different and that really elevates the product above the competition. These are the intersections you need to seek out with a great deal of curiosity, effort and determination.

So innovation, then, lies at the crossroads of three very specific attributes: **desirability**, **feasibility** and **viability**.

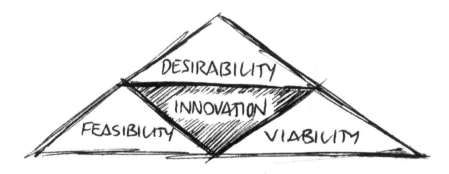

Once again, you start with people, with **desirability**: you may well have a great idea, but does anybody *want* it? Answering that question is very often a highly iterative, unpredictable process. Partly because we're also trying to determine the **feasibility** of creating something that's really high quality:

⇒ Can we create it?

⇒ Can we implement it?

⇒ What's realistic — what can we actually *do*?

⇒ How great can we be within the confines of reality?

And if that weren't enough, we also have to consider the **viability** of the product once it launches:

⇒ What's the *shelf life* of what we're designing?

⇒ How soon before people will be expecting *improvements*?

⇒ How long can we *sustain* that pace?

This balancing act is every bit as challenging as it sounds. But time and effort devoted to strategy, to ***thinking first***, allows us to take quantum leaps forward in creating apps, sites and systems that exceed the expectations of both users and creators.

Thinking first is what allows innovators of any kind to make their dreams and visions reality.

I wrote this book to show you *exactly* how to do that, from the ground up. No matter what your experience or level of formal training, by the time we're done you'll not only know to ask *"why are we doing this?"* — you'll know how to find the **answer**.

Joe Natoli | January 8, 2015

CHAPTER 1

There's No Success Without Strategy

...RATION →

...T IDEA FORWARD
...ACKWARD)

...RATION →

IDEA L→R,
...DUCTIVE IN A
...-OL ENGINEERING

ITERATION
SOLIDIFIES / QUALIFIES
IDEAS

ENSURES YOU DON'T GET
STUCK ON THE WRONG
PATH

...PROVES
"WHAT IF"
SCENARIO...

SOUNDS GREAT — BUT WONT FLY IN
AN AGILE APPROACH ; TWO ARE
DIAMETRICALLY OPPOSED

UXD BUILDING INTERFACES OR SOLVING PROBLEMS ?

"E NEED AN INTERFACE
FOR THIS "

...EDICTABLE DESIGN PROCESS
KNOWN # OF SCREENS
GO U/ FIRST DESIGN GUESS
PREDICTABLE TIME FRAME
EASY TO SCHED. SPRINTS

"WE NEED TO SOLVE
THIS PROBLEM"

UNPREDICTABLE
- COULD TAKE 1 HR TO
  SOLVE A DESIGN PROBLEM
- OR IT COULD TAKE A WEE...
- USABILITY TESTING
  PROVES "FIRST GUESS" IS
  ALMOST ALWAYS WRONG
- DESIGN IS DIFFICULT
  ...

Fail to Plan = Plan to Fail

Decisions that are made on the strategy plane, in particular, have a **massive ripple effect** all the way up the chain. If you screw up on the strategy plane, you'll be paying for it *repeatedly* over the life of the project.

Stop me if you've heard this one before...

Let's say we have in-house UX, IT and Development teams working for a large financial services corporation, which we'll call Acme. Acme is a $2 billion B-to-B enterprise serving 85% of the entire market of brokers, agents and resellers. These folks use the company's web services portal to deliver information and provide analysis tools to their clients.

Now assume that there's a specific **data reporting/analytics feature** the Acme CEO insists must be included. The data set is layered and extremely complex. The UX and IT folks research it and immediately realize they have to seriously re-adjust their design & build strategy. The database architects are raising massive red flags. Their report back essentially says:

> *"There's no way we can build this within budget. It's too complex, it'll take five months longer than we have, there's no way we can ensure the accuracy of the data and it will only work with one of the major web browsers."*

And the Product Manager, VP of Product Development or the CEO, one way or another, says "**I don't care. It has to be in there. Internet Explorer (IE) only.**"

The team begins building, but along the way they realize that they need six additional programmers to pull it off within the timeframe allotted. And not just any programmers, top-shelf, *paid-assassin* type programmers. And they need a CSS whiz who can style all this complex data to make it **understandable by normal human beings**, because the out-of-the-box reporting module produces reports that even a PhD couldn't decipher. They put in a hire request.

The plot thickens

The Acme CEO, and the executive team as a whole, says **NO. Work with what you've got**.

So the team does the only thing they *can* do, since it is physically impossible for them to bend the laws of time and space: **they cut corners**. Everywhere possible. And one of the first things that gets sacrificed is the time and budget allotted for **designing what the reports look like onscreen**.

Despite the corner-cutting, the project is three months late anyway (which everyone on the team knew and said it would be). Customers are getting antsy waiting for this big promised improvement and are beginning to seriously doubt the company's ability to pull it off.

Fast-forward to launch: the product releases, and customers begin using it. And they are immediately, unanimously angry about several things:

1. **They don't know what they're looking at, what it means or how to act on it.** The data presentation is so complex that they can't understand any

of it, much less use it as a basis for critical decision-making.

2. **It doesn't work in their browser.** In their businesses and with their end customers, the web browser used most is Firefox, followed closely by Google Chrome. Neither of which the reporting feature works properly in (as the team predicted).

3. **The numbers don't always add up**. The calculations are often incorrect, and the degree of correctness varies based on the type of report pulled. This is *sensitive financial data*, in some cases representing *million-dollar investments*. You can imagine why this is an issue.

This anger is so profuse and widespread that several of Acme's customers don't renew their contracts. That lost dollar amount is roughly equal to **34% of Acme's yearly revenue**, which, by the way, is measured in **billions**. With a *B*.

All of which makes what I said earlier well worth repeating, particularly for those of you who own businesses or are C-level decision makers:

> **If you screw up on the Strategy Plane, you'll be paying for it repeatedly over the life of the project (and afterward as well).**

The scenario I've just given you isn't too far from hundreds of actual scenarios I've seen over the past two decades. I've had many a spirited discussion with Project Managers, Product Managers, VPs and CEOs over things they insist "just *have* to be done." And I've lost *plenty* of those battles, believe me.

At the end of the day, it's their decision, not mine. It's their money and market share to lose. The only thing I can do is say "here's how that's going to play out" and hope it's given some consideration. And that's all *you* can do as well, if your role is that of a doer instead of a decider.

But if you have a choice — if it's *your* app, *your* website, *your* system — the key to **less stress**, **less suffering** and a **user experience that makes or saves you money** starts with an "S."

I've been privileged to work with some very big, wildly successful organizations over almost three decades, and I can tell you that the one thing they all have in common is this:

> **They spend a great deal of time, effort, resources and *money* on the Strategy Plane of UX.**

As I'm sure you realize from my relentless (bordering on obsessive) hammering of this point in the intro, strategy has the most impact in terms of the success or failure of a product. As I illustrated, there's a ripple effect that happens from the strategy part of the project onward. If you know **what you're building**, if you know **who you're building it for**, and you know **why it's going to be valuable** to those folks (and conversely why it's going to be valuable to *you*), success shall be yours.

As you progress through each plane of UX — from Information Architecture to Interaction Design to User Interface Design — that success goes with you, strengthening your efforts.

However, if you fail to consider all the aspects of product strategy, business strategy and user needs, those miscalculations will *also* follow you through every step of the process. You will find yourself extremely stressed out and very, very frustrated.

What's more, you'll have created something that people will probably not find very useful.

So now that I'm sure you'll never, *ever* forget how intensely important strategy is, I'm going to talk a little about the creation and application of strategy.

Strategy Starts with Research

All good strategy starts with research. Why? Because we don't know everything there is to know about any given problem, or industry, or product, or the people that we're hopefully trying to reach. No matter how long you may have worked in a particular industry or even for a particular client, I guarantee you there is, with every new project, a laundry list as long as your arm of very significant things that you *don't* know.

Research Rule #1

As such, my first rule of research is this: **assume you know nothing**. Let go of every preconception you have; they will only serve to alter your perception of what you're hearing. Objectivity is not impossible; it's actually little more than **learned behavior** that comes from discipline.

For example, even when a client is telling me something I think I already know, I never say "right, I'm aware of that." Instead, I assume there's some part of that story that hasn't been told yet. I assume that either (a) no one has asked them about these things or (b) no one shut their mouths long enough to actually listen to the whole story.

In addition, context changes constantly — especially after I've asked them a number of questions that almost always nudge them into thinking about things they haven't previously. So more often than not, those additional details come out when I remain patient and listen.

And those details are almost always *damn* important.

If I interrupt and indicate this was already covered, those additional details are *never spoken*. So follow rule number one and **assume you know nothing**.

Research Rule #2

And if you ever find yourself doubting rule number one, remember rule number two:

Shut up and listen.

There's More Than One Way

No matter how you go about getting the information and knowledge you don't currently possess, no matter the method or technique, it's **research**. If you are looking for clues into what needs to happen to solve a problem, you are researching. As such, you are now, in fact, a *researcher*.

My point here is that research does not have to be this massive, academic undertaking, where you're taking a very formal, scientific approach to measuring variables and conducting experiments. You do *not* have to subscribe to and practice any number of formalized approaches to UX, design or usability research. Those processes are all extremely relevant and infinitely valuable, but you do not have to have "research skills" in order to do this.

There's no ultimate, single way to do it "right." There are *multiple* ways, means and methods and they all have value. Don't restrict yourself. Be open to whatever means and methods help you meet the goals of the project and the client.

A great deal of user research, for example, starts with simple conversation or direct observation. Talking with your fellow human beings, watching them in action if/when possible and leveraging the tools in front of you. And don't forget one of the most overlooked tools you have: **Google search** (cue trumpets).

There's an awful lot of information to be found via our ubiquitous friend with the funny name. It's beyond easy to find useful (and often validated) information about any given topic, any given audience segment or any given product. In most situations, you will find that there are precedents you can check out and learn from: people looking for the same answers you are, and who have been kind enough to share what they've learned with the rest of us.

So research starts with asking a lot of questions and getting enough answers to either:

1. Confirm that your approach is **appropriate**,

2. Signal that you're on the **wrong path**, or

3. Suggest that you'll need to **do some additional digging** before you'll know for sure.

Start with Stakeholders

The first part of strategic UX research is what we call stakeholder interviews. A stakeholder is any person that has a vested interest in both the product and the outcome.

The stakeholders I'm talking about live on the **business** side of the equation; these are the people who have the most to lose if the product tanks. Every stakeholder has a **specific area of responsibility** related to the product. You need to find out what those areas are and what inherent risks related to those responsibilities exist for each stakeholder.

You find out who those people are — and what exactly they have "at stake" — by answering the questions shown here:

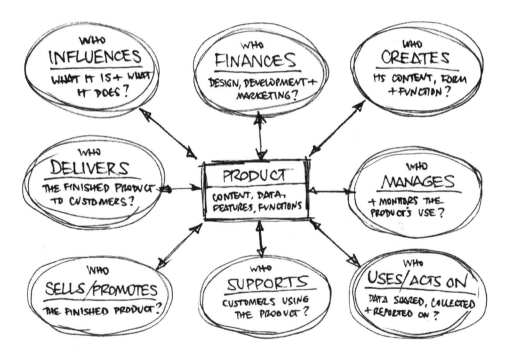

If you're a designer or developer working on a project for a client, then the people that you're talking to might have roles like *Director of Marketing, Director of IT, Product or Project Manager,* etc. These people all have a vested interest in whether this product succeeds or not, all the way up to the level of the CEO or President — the person who's signing the checks to get all of this work done!

These people are all assuming a great deal of **risk**, and as such, are naturally in a position where they can exert great influence over the project (and product). For that reason alone, they are the first group you want to talk to.

You want to know what's on their minds. You want to know what each of them *individually* thinks success is. What has to happen in order for each person to view the effort as successful? Do those definitions apply to more than one person/role? And if they don't, *should* they?

It's important to have these stakeholder conversations/interviews early on, and throughout the project. You want to find out what *everybody* is thinking. If there are differences of opinion about what constitutes success, get them ironed out *before* you start doing any work.

This is critically important. Otherwise you will go down one, two, six or eight paths, and the target will keep moving. You'll be stuck in a situation where nobody can agree on what you're supposed to be doing.

No matter how good you may be, you will find that the target moves **much faster** than you do. As such, you must:

⇒ Talk to **everyone who is in any way connected** to what you're doing.

⇒ Ask **every question** you can possibly think of.

⇒ Do both of those things **early** and **often**.

I'll detail what some of those questions should be, and how they relate to identifying business goals, on page 33. For now, keep all of this in mind.

Next, Move to Users

After stakeholders, you start talking to users. You want to get a representative sample of folks together and ask them a lot of questions about what they like, what they don't like and what they typically do during the day. You want to know about their responsibilities, their critical tasks, their goals and their motivation for achieving those goals. You also want to understand the context of the environment they're operating in:

⇒ If they work in a corporate office, **what policies, processes or procedures** affect
how they do what they do?

⇒ How often do they get **interrupted** during
the day? By who, and for what reason?

⇒ How much time do they spend **in meetings**
instead of at their desks using their computer (or
laptop or tablet)?

The point here is that their *environment* exerts just as much influence — on *what* they do, *why* they do it and *how* they do it — as their personal or professional motivations do.

And again, aside from just interviewing people one on one, the Internet is a treasure trove of information. Because whatever people like or don't like, they get on Facebook, or they get on Twitter, or on Amazon or wherever, and they tell you (and everyone else). And while at one point that public parade of feedback was limited to consumer products, you will now find an equally deep reserve dedicated to B2B products and systems. So even if you can't sit one-on-one with users, you *can* find them. The information is out there.

Walking the walk

From there, it's all analysis and review. You've got answers to all the questions you've asked. You've got transcripts from multiple interesting and illuminating conversations. You've got a ton of stuff that you researched and found online. Now it's time to *look* at all of it and try to figure out what it all means — and how it should inform your UX efforts.

Again, I have to stress that you don't have to use formal processes for doing this analysis. Do they help? Absolutely. If you have experience and tools and processes for formal analysis, by all means take that route. But if you don't, the process is called **read, re-read and take copious notes**.

Once you start reading back everything that you've gathered and collected and noted, you're going to see **patterns**. You'll come across multiple instances where people are *saying* the same thing, *asking* for the same thing, *complaining* about the same thing.

And that activity is what a fancy word like *analysis* really means: looking for patterns in the information you've collected. You want to make note of those things collectively so that they can inform a proposed feature set for the product.

Knowing the need allows you to hypothesize what could be designed to *fill* that need, solve that issue. This, in turn, helps define the scope of what you're doing.

Strategy, Simplicity and Success

Success in the age we're living in — of relentless, widespread complexity — will only come from focusing on **strategic simplicity**. You have to figure out what matters most and strip away everything that doesn't serve that need.

Product success, for the most part, doesn't come from features, functions and underlying code. Widespread product adoption comes from the ways in which we *expose* those features and functions to people who might find them useful. Product sales skyrocket when the experience of use *exceeds* our expectation.

You have to look *past* the hardware, past the languages and platforms and features and extensibility and data. That complexity is self-evident and it's here to stay. But users don't want to know about it. They **don't care** how robust or complex or difficult to control it is. They want simple, and it's entirely up to us as UX, design and technology professionals to make that happen.

The key to doing so, the tipping point, the ace in the deck, the silver bullet – call it whatever you want – is a relentless focus on answering people's need for simplicity in the user experience.

Why? Because more complexity under the hood demands more simplicity and ease of use in the driver's seat.

Do the research. Ask a *lot* of questions. Solve the *right* problems.

Research doesn't have to be complicated, and it doesn't matter so much how you go about collecting and analyzing data. It matters more that you take the time to **do it** — and that you steadfastly refuse to **skip it**.

CHAPTER 2

Identifying Business Goals

OUTSIDE WORLD

REST OF THE COMPANY
(LOCAL, NAT'L, GLOBAL)

DEPT./BIZ UNIT
PRODUCT SERVES

PRODUCT

IMPACT
OF POSITIVE
OR NEGATIVE
UX/CX SPANS
ALL AREAS OF
THE ORGANIZAT'
(+ BEYOND)

PRODUCT DEV.

DESIGN

DEV'T

CUST. SVC.

SALES

MKTG.

EXECS

OPERATIONS

IT

HR

CUSTOMERS

PARTNERS

SUPPLIERS

GOV'T REGULATORS

UX Means *Business*

Before we dive into the details, I want to say this: the core concern of any commercial entity is money. And as such, every business goal relates back to doing one of two things:

1. *Making* money
2. *Saving* money

Do companies care about customers? Yes. Does this mean all businesses are essentially bloodthirsty vampires? No. Aren't we also here to make people's lives easier, to give them value and delight? Of course.

But right now we're talking about **business goals**. And the bottom line is this:

> **It is exceedingly difficult to stay in business if you are unable to effectively, continually make and/or save money.**

It just isn't any more complicated than that. Your primary job as a Designer, UXer or Developer is to help these people either make money or save it.

Conducting Stakeholder Interviews

Business goals come primarily from the folks who are carrying the most *responsibility* and *risk* for the project's success: the **stakeholders**. These are the folks we talked about in the preceding section. They are your project/product owners, your subject matter experts. They are the people who can explain to you what success means, both for the business and for them.

Which means that in addition to wanting to know how a product redesign will affect the business, you also want to know how it's going to affect each of those people — and their departments if it's a large organization — individually. Think:

⇒ Who has **decision-making authority** (and who doesn't)?

⇒ Who has the most to **gain** or **lose**?

⇒ What happens to each person's world if the project **succeeds**?

⇒ What happens if it **fails**?

Always remember that success for one stakeholder *may not be the same as success for another*. And should those goals be diametrically opposed, you may find yourself caught in the middle of a political battle.

If that happens, you'll need to know how lightly to tread.

You also want to be able to recognize when you're **fighting a losing battle** that will only end in tragedy for all involved. I've been involved with a few of those projects. They last *forever* — and the mental and emotional stress lasts even longer.

So one of the first critical things you have to do is get the lay of the land; find out where each stakeholder is coming from and what they expect to happen.

Asking the Right Questions

In some cases you will be in a room with a lot of sharp people who already know they need to give you a thorough tour of what they're doing and why. But in many cases, **you'll need to ask for details**. Because quite often, they may not understand *why* you need to know something. So unless you ask, they may never share some mission-critical knowledge.

The questions you ask, obviously, should be specific to the client's business model, market, product, industry, etc. But there are more than a handful of questions that you should ask of **every business stakeholder**, **every time**. Here are the most important of those:

1. **Who are your customers or users?** You want to get to know the people that use this product or service *right now.* What do they do with the product? What do they like about it? What do they expect from it?

   This is where, if possible, you want to involve folks who work in the call center or are directly responsible for interfacing with customers (e.g. sales people). You want to know what customers complain about and how often. And you also want to know if the organization can draw a straight line from any of those complaints to lost revenue, or to customers choosing a competitor.

   You also want to know more about these people as individuals, about their responsibilities and motivations. You also want to get the business' take on the people that use their product. Coupled with user interviews, this will often reveal a gap the size of the Grand Canyon between what the business *thinks* customers do or want and what those customers *really* do or want.

2. **What business goal should the end product serve — what should it *do* for the business?** What needs to happen once we launch (or re-launch) this and people *use* it? How does each person in the room define success? How will each person (and their department) **measure** that success? The measurement part matters a great deal, because any goal that can't be measured is one that probably can't be **achieved**. And even if it can, no one will know when that's happened.

You want to know *why* the company is rolling out this new product or service, or why you're being asked to redesign what exists now. Those "whys" are business goals:

⇒ Will the new features and functions **convince more customers to pay** for the product/service?

⇒ **Will it convince them to pay more than they're paying now**, or make a case for adding additional upgrades?

⇒ Will a better product keep them from **switching to a competitor**?

⇒ Is this product intended to **replace an existing, outdated legacy system** that's too expensive to maintain and riddled with inefficiency?

3. **What role does this product play in the company's overall business strategy?** No man is an island, and inside a business, no project is either. Among all the things the organization does, there will be multiple pieces that will impact what you're doing. You need to know what those things are so that they don't sneak up and derail you later.

In heavily regulated industries, for example, changes to the law can have a profound effect on how data is collected, accessed, manipulated and stored. Whatever you're proposing has to be in line with those external constraints. So you want to be sure you ask:

→ Are there any **company-wide initiatives or mandates** that could affect this product in any way?

→ Are there any **changes to current business processes** that dictate how the product will be managed from an administrative perspective?

→ You want to know the flipside of that one as well: are there any **planned features, functions or services** in the works that may force the company to modify — or even reinvent — **current processes** and procedures?

4. **What technology is in place, and what related technology decisions have already been made?**

This is tremendously important, especially with established organizations who will typically have an IT department in charge of all of the technology decisions that get made. Those people must be at the table from day one.

For all you know, they may say, "*look, we don't care what you build but it must work in a Microsoft IIS environment. We absolutely will not support PHP or any open source products or platforms.*" **Security** plays a part here as well; every organization has different security requirements and many have a large investment in an established infrastructure. And no matter how brilliant you may be, *none of that* is changing for your project.

The existing parameters around technology have a profound impact in what you recommend, design and ultimately build. As such, make sure IT is present and accounted for, and **ask this question up front**, *every time*. Otherwise you may be in for a big surprise in 3 months, part of which includes a very angry client who was looking to *you* to figure out all this "techie" stuff.

5. **Why do you think customers would use this specific product?** An obvious question, to be sure. But believe it or not, in the mad rush of day-to-day pressures, tasks and activities inside a corporation, it's

not often that people step back to ask *"why do customers care about this?"*

The act of doing so often prompts people to re-examine their preconceptions. I've been in rooms where after 40 minutes of what sounded like a solid list of reasons, the conversation dissolves into twelve people thinking *WOW...we thought we knew, but, er...ah...maybe we don't know.*

I also want you to notice how **open-ended** the question is. That's on purpose. You're purposely leaving a very large gap that the ensuing conversation will fill in.

And in most cases, some incredibly important things will come to light in that gap.

Addressing the competition

Once you've spoken to stakeholders about their issues, opinions and business goals, it's time to direct your efforts toward the competition. Although much of the conversation up to this point will have referenced competitors, now is the time to address it explicitly and in detail. That means identifying competing products, services and companies.

Some of these will be **direct** competitors, meaning they offer the exact same set of products and services your client (or your business) does.

Others will be **indirect** competitors, meaning that they offer some of what your client or company offers, but there may be other offerings they have that you don't, or vice versa.

If you ever hear the words "we have no competition," that's your cue to exit. Any and *every* organization has competition, direct or not. And no matter how new or unique a new business may be, you (and they) have to keep in mind that the world is a big place — and the Internet has given us access to every corner of it. Your competitors are at your doorstep. And even if they're not outside at the moment, I assure you they are en route.

If you know what the competition is doing well (and what they're *not*) it'll be easier to identify areas where competitive advantage can be created. Here are the most common, and most *important*, questions to ask about competitors.

1. **Who are your top five competitors?** As with the "no competition" clause above, anyone who can't name five competitors is woefully misinformed. So press the issue, and encourage them to think about indirect competitors, Of those competitors, you want to know:

   ⇒ How many have a legitimate shot at **stealing your current or potential customers**? Why?

   ⇒ If someone really *can* steal your thunder, what do you think you need to do **to prevent that** from happening?

2. **What are the primary differences between your business model and theirs?** How do they make money, and how do *you* make money? The degree to which those methods are **alike** determine just how dangerous those competitors are. And how

important your UX efforts will be. Because in a situation where companies are fighting for the *exact same customers* with the *exact same services*, **most traditional areas of differentiation will be of no use to you (or them)**.

What typically happens is that organizations compete on things like price or feature set, because everything else is so similar. Problem is, neither approach really works. What I tell clients is this:

> **In apples-to-apples competitive situations, the only thing that really determines who gets more customers is *how easy you make it for people to do business with you.***

The typical "we're cheaper" approach goes right out the window if using your services involves multiple calls or chats with customer service, frequent browser errors, unintuitive labeling and a level of effort that demands a quarter of or more of someone's workday.

3. **If people use a competitor's product instead of yours, what's the reason?** They may not *know* the exact reason. Or they may know and are uncomfortable talking about it. But nine times out of ten, I think you'll find that if a company is getting pounded by the competition, if it's rapidly losing market share, they know — or at least *suspect* — why.

   It may be a very *difficult* why, but it's there. Otherwise you wouldn't be in the room in the first place.

In terms of market share and revenue, you need to know whether they are:

(a) Holding their own,

(b) far ahead, or

(c) **getting their asses kicked**.

Because if it turns out to be (c), you'll need to do some additional digging to make sure you understand why that's happening.

At this point in history, nearly every service in almost every industry is delivered via technology. And **when that technology is hard to use, people bail**. They will gladly pay another provider *more* if that product places less demand on their time or effort.

4. **What's your strategy in terms of positioning and differentiating this product?** Essentially what you're asking here is *"Why you?"* What's going to be different about this product, and will that difference be (a) **obvious** and (b) **meaningful** to customers? Specifically, you want to dig into what that difference really is:

  ⇒ Is it a **massive, large-scale difference** that's obvious in three seconds, or is it only visible once you dive down into specs and details?

→ What are the **core differences** between this product's feature set and that of the competition?

→ **What's the one thing they're *not* giving customers that you can?** Or vice versa?

What you want to get a handle on is simple: **what are competitors doing, and is it working?** Do people like it? Do they hate it? Is the Internet chatter praising or complaining?

The complaint part is very valuable to you, by the way: if you can find examples of features and functions that people routinely complain about in the competition's products, those can often be areas you can capitalize on. You've got an opportunity to say to your users "*we know you hate this kind of thing, so we don't do that*."

That's low-hanging fruit — an obvious opportunity for differentiation — and it should absolutely be part of your plan.

Evaluating Answers (When to Keep Asking Questions)

You want **specific, measurable answers**, and you have to keep pressing until you get them. The measurable part is important here — because If you can't measure something, you probably can't achieve or manage it. Why? Because **you'll never know if you've *reached* it** .

Specific, measurable answers should sound something like this:

→ *"We want to cut the time it takes customers to sign up by at least 30%."*

→ *"We want to cut the number of calls to our call center in half within six months."*

→ *"We want to decrease our shopping cart abandonment to less than 3%."*

Those kinds of answers point to the places you need to begin looking at in order to understand the problem. The more specific the goal, the easier it is to figure out what kinds of things will contribute to reaching it.

Pushing for specific answers like these also goes a long way in avoiding an all-too-common situation where you've got a lot of people on a team and none of them see the project the same way. They have very *different* ideas about what success means, very different ideas about what needs to be done.

What's more, **each person has very different motivations** for their perceived goal. Some of those motivations are personal, some are political, and some are directly related to the harsh reality of someone simply trying to hang on to his or her job. You want to uncover as much of that motivation as possible so that you can properly frame each person's input.

A good friend of mine related a story awhile back that has always stuck with me. It's a simple, understated exchange or words that on the surface may not seem like much. In reality, however, its the equivalent of an ear-splitting air raid siren, warning you that you are headed into dangerous territory. And it also suggests that there are more than a few questions to be answered. Here's how the story goes:

Years back, my colleague was partnering with an IT firm, building a services portal for a large financial services client. The IT firm was handling all aspects of design & build; my friend was on board as a consultant. During that time they had dozens of conversations that went like this:

CEO: How long will it take you to make this feature list reality?

PM: This is a long, complex list. We need 14 months, at bare minimum. And to be honest, we're not convinced that our current server environment will support *half* of what's on this list.

CEO: WHAT!?! No. No way we can wait that long. This has to be live in *six months*.

PM: OK.

Some of you are shocked, and some of you are laughing knowingly. This happens more often than any of us would care to admit. The Project Manager immediately caved in to the CEO's demand, despite the fact that (a) the delivery date was **logistically impossible** and (b) **absolutely nothing** in that exchange of words made the CEO's deadline any more achievable.

When that deadline wasn't met, the project ended in disaster. The IT firm was subsequently fired, and the resulting bad blood was hard on everyone.

So when you're in this situation, in my colleague's shoes or the Project Manager's shoes — or just an observer — you want to push for a much more realistic approach and outcome. In other words, ask more questions, such as:

⇒ **What is the worst thing that happens if we don't deliver by this date?** You're trying to find out whether the proposed schedule is actually driven by a specific event or consequence, instead of personal fear or desire. Or by the knee-jerk need to answer everything with "ASAP."

⇒ **If the date can't move, which features & functions absolutely have to be in place by then?** More often than not, everyone will come to the realization that only *certain* things have to be accomplished in the initial time frame. And that having those features in place and working will buy the team more time for everything else.

⇒ **Can we get more time, money or resources?** Can we expand the budget to hire a few additional people? Are there internal folks we can pull from other projects to help us? Will expanding the schedule by two weeks cause any major consequences? Something has to give; you have to figure out what that is.

⇒ **Does it have to work or look perfect by that date?** Quality is another thing that can be sacrificed (within reason) in a compressed time frame. Consider what things users may overlook if they get something else in the meantime.

To wrap this up, I'd like to share something I heard a consultant say almost a decade ago. It's always stuck with me, because it's one of the best pieces of advice I've ever received:

Silence equals agreement.

If you say nothing about something you think is not possible, or that you believe is dangerous, you are not only agreeing that it's the right thing to do — you are also agreeing to *do it*.

CHAPTER 3

Identifying User Needs

WHICH CHOICE
IS THE RIGHT
ONE?

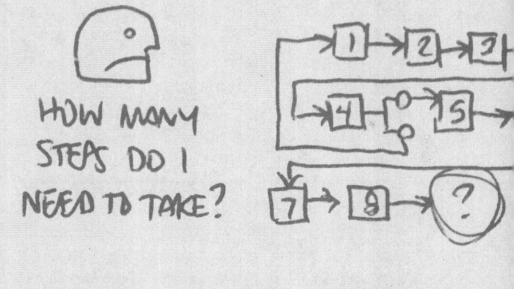

HOW MANY
STEPS DO I
NEED TO TAKE?

HOW LONG WILL
EACH STEP TAKE
TO COMPLETE?

Identifying Business-to-Business (B2B) User Needs

So once we know what the business goals are for the product, now it's time to figure out what people (a.k.a. **users**) want from it. What are they after and what do they expect? What's the **value** delivered to them in this equation?

Remember, User Experience is a **value loop**: if value goes out to the people who use the product, it's highly likely that value will come back to the creator, the organization, the investor sponsoring the product. Value out equals value back in.

In the realm of commercial use, users are split into two segments. The first of those is **Business-to-Business (B2B)**. In a B2B situation, whatever it is that you're designing or building specifically addresses and enables business tasks and activities. The people who use it do so to further business activities — their own or those of their employer.

If you're creating a time and attendance system, for example, your users are employees required by their employer to fill out a timesheet every week. When we're talking about B2B users, there's a different tack you need to take in talking to them about their roles, responsibilities and needs.

Asking the Right Questions

Asking the right questions starts with the actual **form** of the questions you ask. These should be open-ended, non-leading, non-specific questions that let the person fill in the details of the answer. You don't necessarily ask them about what software or hardware they use; you ask them what they *do*, how they would complete a task.

That means you *don't* ask a question like *"what part of this application do you use to do Task X?"*

Why? Because that question focuses on the **tool** the person is using — instead of the **process** they go through. And as I said previously, it's the process that matters most.

There are any number of factors unrelated to the specific software, hardware or even the task at hand that are contributing to the current issue or problem. And if you ask a narrow question that's tactic- or tool-specific, you'll never hear about any of them.

Usability and UX problems are very rarely the sole result of a technology issue; there are a handful of other seemingly unrelated factors that, in many cases, turn out to be the real problem: company policies, processes, politics, deadlines, stress, noise, interruptions, etc.

So again, if you only ask a user about the software she's using, **you won't get any information about the other factors that may be directly responsible for the issues at hand**.

The software may very well suck — but if there's a process or policy in place that doesn't allow that person enough time or give them the right data to do their job, **that's the *real* issue**.

The only way you can address the real issue is if you *know* about it. And if you don't know about it, the person and the organization will still have the same problem after the redesign launches or your engagement is over.

Not only is that bad for the organization, it's bad for you too, because in the organization's eyes they've just invested a great deal of time and money on... well... *nothing*.

The right question, then, looks like this:

"Walk me through how you would complete Task X."

Now, that person may tell you about another system or website (or two or three) they use in order to get additional information before they act. They may explain how they have to make three phone calls to *three different departments* to get additional information before doing anything. They may explain how they wind up using their mobile phone instead of their desktop machine because they're stuck in meetings for more than half their workday.

Along the way, when they volunteer information you find interesting or surprising, you simply prompt for more detail by asking *"why do you do that?"*

The goal is to uncover **what they use** (especially if there are multiple tools involved) and what aspects of those things help or hinder what they're doing. You're looking to build a picture of what's going to meet their needs the best. And to do that you need information. Not only about how they use something, but how they go about their day, what their *motivations* are.

You want to know why these tasks — and completing them in a certain way — is important. You want to know what they *expect* to accomplish and why it matters to them.

Throughout the process, remain focused on the **why**, the motivation. The desired result. Is accomplishing Task X going to make them look good to their boss? Is accomplishing Task Y going to save them time? Is accomplishing both X and Y going to make them richer? Taller? Better looking?

Whatever it is, you need to know about it.

Here are some questions you should always ask of B2B users:

1. **How do you define a successful work day? What has to happen in order for you to feel good when you leave?** At the end of the day, what makes that person feel like they were productive, like they got things accomplished? What things happen that give the person that impression? The opposite question is valuable as well: what kinds of things make you feel unproductive? Frustrated?

2. **How do you go about doing X?** This can be any number of things that they do during the course of a normal work day. For example, if the product you've been asked to design is a time and attendance system, you might ask the person, *"How do you usually go about filling out your time sheet? Walk me through that process."* You may hear something like:

   > *"I type in my hours and hand my timesheet to my boss. He has to approve it, and if something's wrong or he doesn't agree, he gives it back to me and tells me what to change. If it's approved it goes to Anne in HR, who has to approve it, and from there it goes to Accounting because they have to bill the client for my time."*

   In three sentences, this person has just given you intel on a **probable workflow** and the **people it may need to notify** when events occur.

In other words, you're getting **requirements** — just by having a simple conversation. From the previous answer, for example, you now know that:

→ Three other people have to **view** and **approve** what the user submits.

→ If it's incorrect, the approver needs the ability to **add a comment** explaining what needs to be fixed (and why).

→ The user needs the ability to **modify** their entries and **re-submit.**

→ Each time one of the parties approves the timesheet, the next party in the chain needs to be **notified** that it's ready for their review.

→ It may need to be **integrated** with an existing accounting system where hours and project codes can be imported and populated on an invoice.

This is how useful, valuable requirements are created. Instead of picking them out of the air or mimicking existing systems, you start with people: who they are, what they do and what needs to happen as a result.

3. **Did you do this (task) in the same way at other organizations you've worked for? Was it better, worse or different?** Most people have worked for

more than one company, so they will likely have experienced variations on a theme — different ways of doing the same thing. Some may be worse than the current scenario. But hearing what was *better* may give you some ideas about improving what they're using now.

4. **What are the biggest problems, obstacles or inefficiencies you deal with?** What are the things that prevent people from being efficient or make them do more work than they feel is necessary? What grinds productivity to a halt and stops everyone in their tracks?

Let's stick with the time and attendance example. If you're talking to someone in Accounting, you may very well hear:

> *"People hate doing their timesheets because the system's so hard to use, so they do them late. When that happens, the end result is that invoices go out late, which causes stress all the way down the line from Accounting to HR to the Department heads. Everyone is hounding the next person in line to get the employee to turn in their timesheet!*
>
> *And clients get upset because getting their invoice late screws up the flow of their internal bill payment cycle. So one simple act causes a lot of conflict and adversity for us; it makes everything tense all the time here."*

You're looking for the **underlying causes** of issues, errors, backlogs. Again, notice that you're not asking or discussing the software itself.

You just heard that there's a consistent problem here: *people turn their timesheets in late*. So now you need to find out, in as much detail as possible, *why* people wait until the last minute to do their timesheets. The answer — the *why* — will tell you what features and functions you can design to help solve this problem.

5. **Can you tell me about all the other systems that work with this one?** In the business world, you will *never* find an instance where one single system handles everything the organization needs to do on a daily basis. From the email system to the Intranet to the Project Management software to the CRM platform to the CMS that runs the client portal to the Accounting & Billing software... you see where I'm going with this? Separate applications, separate systems, separate users.

As such, the things that get *shared* between those systems — and how well or how poorly that sharing happens — have a big impact on user and customer experience. The design decisions you make related to features and functions will directly impact the other systems your app talks to — and may cause problems for those users as well. So in order to make good decisions you need to know what those other systems are and how they work.

This is the time where you **make sure there is a representative from IT at the table**. And if there isn't, there better be one on your team. Not addressing interoperability properly can paint you in a corner frighteningly fast.

Identifying Business-to-Consumer (B2C) User Needs

If the product in question is used directly by consumers, then we're talking about **Business-to-Consumer (B2C)**. Anything sold via Amazon.com, for example, is a B2C product because it goes directly to consumers. Google Play, iTunes, Spotify and the like all sell B2C products.

The questions for B2C users are necessarily different. We're not going to ask them about daily work habits or company-mandated goals and assignments. We're not asking them about the company that they're a part of, either. Why? Because those factors have a lot less influence on their buying or use decisions.

Asking the Right Questions

The approach, once again, should be open-ended; no leading questions. No matter what the app or site or system is meant to help them figure out — what their shoe size is, for example — you start big and simple.

Your role here is not to solve problems or suggest solutions, it's to get **unbiased information**. So don't give them advice or try to push them in any particular direction. Just let them answer the question and *listen*.

Open-ended questions often prompt silence, which allows people the necessary space to walk you through the answer. So patience is extremely important here; let the silence following the question do the heavy lifting, and repress the urge to fill it with your own voice.

Here are some examples of open-ended questions:

1. **What part of this do you hate doing?** What's the part of this process that you know is coming, but that you're really dreading? Is there a part you wish you didn't have to do?

   For instance, if you're talking to somebody about a checkout process on an ecommerce site, they may absolutely loathe the common disconnects of entering credit card information. You may hear:

   > *"Well, I really hate entering my credit card because I always have to figure out which number corresponds with which month. They're never labeled the same as what's on the card! I mean, the card says 10 and the droplist says October, and I actually have to count in my head to figure out what month I need to choose on the screen. Every. Single. Time."*

   That answer, especially if echoed by a significant number of other people, gives you a clue that mimicking the format on the card, or including the month's corresponding number, might yield measurable improvement.

2. **What frustrates you most about this?** What makes you think *"ARRRRGH!! Why do I even have to **do** this?"* For instance, people often complain when they have to enter in any sort of identifying account information more than once. That's because in most instances (a) they've already been asked for it and (b) they expect the system to have it already.

   So they may say:

   > *"Why does the person who answers in the call center ask me for all the information I just spent 15 minutes keying in after the voice prompts??"*

   Or you may hear:

   > *"Why the hell do I have to give you my username again when I start the checkout process? I already gave it to you when I logged in!!"*

   Those are the kinds of things that you'll hear when you ask that question. And when these answers are near-unanimous, they represent opportunities to deliver UX greatness. Or to alert the client that there are Customer Experience problems that need to be addressed, in areas *outside* the technology and/or the product.

3. **How often do you use this product (or tool)?** If you're creating something altogether new, the question might be *"how often do you use this kind*

of product?" How often do you come to this site? How often do you open this app?" In this case, you're looking to learn something about **frequency of use**. And that tells you something about how valuable the product is.

If it's used often, it's probably become part of that person's daily life. And if it's part of that person's life, it's pretty important to find out what's good or bad about it.

4. **What do you use it to do?** Quite often, you'll find that someone is using an app or site in a way that's slightly (and often radically) different than what it was designed to do. This, again, is an opportunity to uncover potential features you may never otherwise have thought of.

   Google, for example, is essentially a search engine. You go there and you search the Internet. But there are a lot of people for whom *Google IS the Internet*. As such, these folks will go to the search bar on the Google main screen and type in a full URL, *www.givegoodux.com*, instead of typing it in the address bar in the browser. For them, Google is the **one and only way** you use the Internet.

   It's really important to ask this question — because the answer may be a far cry from what you expect.

5. **Can you show me how you do that?** When the interviewee is explaining, *"I do this, and then I do this and then I look at this in order to...,"* ask them

to **show you** how that happens. Here's why: what people *say* they do isn't always a perfect match for what they *actually* do. So by observing the actual action, you may also pick up on a few things that they're not verbalizing.

You may watch them struggle to press a key combination, or you may watch them wander around the screen before they can find the link that they're supposed to click on. Those little things you see will tell you an awful lot in addition to what you're hearing. When it comes to user behavior, seeing is most definitely believing.

6. **What other things do you do (or use) before, during or after you use this product?** Nothing is used in a vacuum, so a lot of times there will be something that they're doing *before* they open your app, and then there may also be some consistent task that they perform *after* they use your app with a different tool. If that's happening, you want to know what those other tools or products are.

Adobe, for example, made some critical changes to its InDesign page layout software after learning about how Designers were using it. Adobe learned that the process of **editing an embedded image** was cumbersome; you had to go back to the source file, open and edit it in Photoshop or Illustrator, then go back to InDesign and update the image. Multiple steps, lots of time lost.

Adding an *Edit Original* option when right-clicking the image streamlined that workflow. If I right-click on an image in my book layout, I get this:

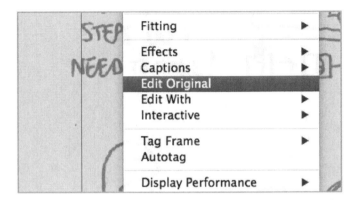

Clicking *Edit Original* **opens the image in its native application** automatically, and, once it's saved, InDesign **updates the image** automatically.

Removing a few steps felt like a quantum leap in simplicity for designers — and more importantly, they felt like Adobe was *listening*. They felt like Adobe understood their needs and cared enough to *do something* about it. That's how **loyalty** is both created and cemented.

So if users are supplementing your app with a few others, it may very well be because those apps do things **they wish yours did**, and they may also wish there was more interoperability between them.

These are critical points of identification that open the door to determining what features and functionality will really make an impact, increase use and improve experience.

7. **Are there other systems you've used that are similar to this one?** What you're asking here is "*how does this system stack up against other things that do the same thing (or similar things)?*" If there's no direct comparison to be had, you might ask:

→ **What are the top three sites or apps that you use on a regular basis?** Which do you return to time and time again?

→ **Can you see this app becoming part of your daily routine?** Why or why not?

This holistic approach will give you some insight as to what recurring, useful role your product or service could play in the person's life. And that insight should be considered within the context of *all the other things* that they're doing.

Questions Specific to Redesign Projects

A significant chunk of the work you'll do as a designer or developer will be **redesigning** something that already exists. You'll be helping to roll out version 2.0 of the app or version 4.1 of the website or version 6.7 of the internal timekeeping system.

In these cases, in addition to your interviews, you want to ask questions that essentially create an audit of the existing product.

That just means asking the same questions covered in the preceding sections — except this time around, you're asking them to frame their answers within the **context of using the existing product**. In this case, their experience up to now is very useful for informing what needs to change or be improved.

So when you're talking to **stakeholders**, you'll mainly be asking questions about how the current version of product impacts business and customer support activities. In addition to how useful the outcome has been. Here are some examples:

1. **What occurrences or information led you to believe a redesign was needed?** What was the catalyst that made everyone wake up and say "*we have to do something about this*?"

2. **What usage data, analytics or customer/partner feedback do you have that you can share?** Do you have data that helps illustrate the problem?

3. **What do you believe a redesign will do for the business?** In other words, what will happen that's *not* happening now?

4. **What criticisms or complaints do your salespeople hear most frequently?** What issues do they spend the majority of their time discussing or trying to solve?

5. **What complaints do you or your call center hear the most?** Do those issues prevent people from a successful outcome with the product?

With **users**, you ask everything in the preceding section, along with questions like:

1. **Are you currently using another product (or process) to do things that this one doesn't?** If the software is lacking, how do you get around its feature/function limitations?

2. **Have you used another product to do the same thing?** If so, was it better or worse than this one?

3. **What features here act as obstacles to you?** What do they keep you from doing or accomplishing, and in what way?

4. **What features and functions do you think could be better?** What's close to what you need, but falls short of either your expectation or your anticipated/expected outcome?

5. **How would those improvements help you?** Would you be more efficient? Would you save time? Would it help you win the affections of the opposite sex?

OK, so maybe you skip that last question.

Unless, of course, your client happens to be an online dating or matchmaking service.

CHAPTER 4

Three Critical Questions You *Must* Ask

PRODUCT TEAMS   PRODUCT MANAGER

BOARD

CEO

CMO   COO   CTO   CIO   HR

VP   VP   VP   VP   MGR

MGR   MGR   MGR   MGR

                     VP
                     PROD,
                     DSN

                     MGR

· DOES:

MARKET RESEARCH
PRODUCT DEFINITION   WHOSE ASS IS   WHO LOSE
DESIGN   ON THE LINE   THE MOST
PROTOTYPE ENGINEERING   MOST ?   UX CALLS
PRODUCTION   SD

WHO HAS MOTIVATION TO

No matter the industry, niche or product type, a core component of developing solid product strategy is asking three crucial, universal questions. Years ago I attended an Adaptive Path seminar where the presenter introduced three critical questions tied to positive UX and product value. I became a believer on the spot, taking *furious* notes. I have *insisted* on asking these same questions of my clients for the last 26 years. Whether you're building something from the ground up or redesigning an existing product, your marching orders are the same at this point:

⇒ You need to find out **what's worth doing**.

⇒ You need to have a shared understanding of **what you're creating**.

⇒ You need to be absolutely sure everyone understands (and agrees on) what **value it delivers**.

One: What's Worth Doing?

We've got a handle on what the business needs, along with an understanding of what users need. Now, from all of that we've researched, from all that we've heard from stakeholders and users, we want to determine:

⇒ **What can be accomplished within the bounds of reality?** What are we certain we can actually achieve, meaning both tasks and outcomes?

⇒ **What's worth the organization's investment in the project?** Will everything on our list result in value back to the organization?

⇒ **What's worth *our* time and investment in the project?** Will the things we do deliver value to users and to the business, or are they band-aids on gaping wounds?

The answers to those questions are determined by figuring out what the tradeoffs are between the product's **importance** and its **feasibility/viability**. This graph illustrates the relationship between the two.

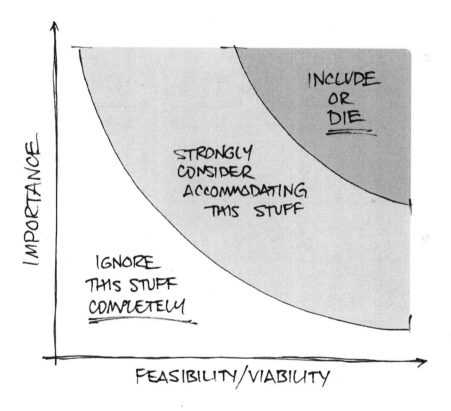

On one axis you have **importance**. How important is the product as a whole — to the business, to users, to achieving the intended end goals? Individual features and functions, and the degrees to which they fulfill needs and deliver value, also have to be weighed and considered here.

The corresponding axis represents **feasibility** and **viability**. Here, we plot the answers to questions such as:

⇒ What can we reasonably accomplish with the **budget** and **resources** (read: people) we currently have available?

⇒ How much of the **anticipated workload** can we conceivably do in the time that we have allocated to us?

⇒ If we do get the work done and the product launches, how will we continue to **maintain and improve** it post-launch?

Anything that lands in the **lower left** section is *out*. As in immediately. If a proposed feature is of low importance and it's highly unlikely that you can do it with the constraints that you have, then you do one of two things:

1. If you're working on an **existing product**, you **postpone any UX improvements** to the features in question for a later release, or

2. If you're working on a **new product**, you **scrap those features altogether**. And if you're evaluating the product as a whole, you scrap it and go do something else.

You never want to waste time or money addressing things that (a) aren't **important** and (b) probably aren't **possible**.

Features that fall in the **middle section** of the graph should be accommodated, but you shouldn't spend the majority of your effort doing so. Anything that lands here is likely less than critical for both the users and the business — and it's also likely you've got some doubts as to whether you can pull them off in the first place.

So these are things that, despite your perfectionist tendencies, simply **don't have to be the best they can be**. Sometimes, as a friend of mine likes to say, *"the most perfect something ever has to be is **done**."*

Anything that falls in that **top right area** is of high importance and high feasibility. That means you're damn sure it's *important* and you're equally damn sure you can *do it*.

These are the **sweet spot**s, the things that are going to provide real, measurable value to all players. It's well worth your time to make sure those things are not only incorporated but that they are designed extremely well, that they shine extremely bright in terms of the value that they provide.

These are the things that enable the product to serve as an **answer to a prayer**.

As such, that's where the majority of your UX, design and development effort should be spent — because that's where the **value** is, for both you and your users/customers. That's where you'll get the most return on your effort.

Two: What Are We Creating?

There's an old joke about how disconnects happen between a project team. Essentially it illustrates how miscommunication

HOW THE CLIENT EXPLAINED IT

HOW THE SALES PERSON UNDERSTOOD IT

HOW THE PROJECT MGR. UNDERSTOOD IT

HOW THE DESIGNER DESIGNED IT

HOW THE DEVELOPER CODED IT

WHAT THE CLIENT REALLY NEEDED

takes place across each member of team. It's a universal example that has been applied to nearly every industry, a story that's been told and re-told millions of times.

Aside from being simultaneously painful and hilarious to those of us who've experienced it, there's also a critically important **moral** to the story: **when everyone isn't on the same page, the end result satisfies *no one.***

The illustration on the opposite page tells one version of this tale. Obviously, there were some massive gaps in communication here, resulting in very different ideas about what the **end result** was supposed to be. Now, while this is an extreme way of representing this idea, it's not really all that uncommon. In fact, it's actually pretty easy for people to wind up with apples when the discussion is about oranges.

One very big reason for this is the fact that **we all have our own languages**, and our own variants of that language. And I don't just mean our ethnic backgrounds; I mean the ways in which our experiences shape our **understanding** of things we see, hear, or read. Cultural preconceptions — our mental models and reflexive associations about the way things work — are applied to everything we see, hear and do.

If you describe an object to six people, they'll all likely know what it is. But each person's **mental image** of it and related **associations** about what it *looks like* or how it *feels* or what it *does* may be very different.

As such, it's not uncommon for everyone to walk away from the table thinking slightly differently about what they're all trying to accomplish — and what it's going to take to get there.

When everyone is not on the same page, the end result will satisfy no one. This lack of common understanding derails projects at frightening speed. And in my experience, that derailment is **extremely difficult to recover from** once it happens.

So the questions in the preceding sections need to be asked of every single person involved in the project. And the answers need to be documented and shared in some form.

Specifications, requirements, formal documents or email; it doesn't matter how you do it or how you share it. But whatever the common understanding of the feature set and required functionality is, it needs to be **available** and **understandable** to every person involved.

And we're not just talking about software specs. Every player also has to have a common understanding of what the **content** is, along with where's it going to come from and who's going to create and approve it. That means everything from statistical data to marketing content to images, audio or video.

Part of your job is to make sure that everyone at the table is in agreement. You want shared understanding of the **project goals**, along with what needs to be designed and built in order to *meet* those goals.

And above all else, you want to make sure that your discussions address the **why**, in addition to the **what**.

Taking the time to dig in deep during the strategy phase will pay dividends over and over as the project progresses. You will find that the subsequent phases will run much more smoothly, and the very next question will be easier to answer.

Three: What Value Does It Deliver?

That, as you might imagine, is a pretty big question. The good news is that there are a series of smaller questions that can help you answer it.

1. **Who is our target audience?** Down to the most specific detail we can uncover, *who's going to use this thing*? Are they male or female? Are they of specific ethnic descent? Do they have a specific job role and responsibility?

   For example, assume that research thus far indicates that our typical user is an African-American pastry chef, working for an independent bakery. She is most likely female and anywhere from thirty-five to forty-five years old. The more **detail** you can put around this user, the more specific you can get about who she is, what her environment is like and how that affects her assumptions, expectations and behavior. That makes it easier to answer the next question, which is...

2. **What experiences are valuable to them?** Let's say that the product you're designing is a mobile app for a Blackberry wholesaler. This wholesaler — along with the Blackberry industry as a whole — has a vested interest in these pastry chefs because they are directly responsible for their bakery's fruit purchases. They are the gatekeepers to profit.

   After interviewing 30 African-American pastry chefs, let's say we've discovered that there is currently no way for them to monitor the status of their fruit shipments in real-time. That's important because their ability to compete is dependent on their ability to schedule production accurately and meet shipping deadlines to restaurants.

So we come up with the idea to provide real-time shipment tracking via text alerts to their mobile phones (they're busy, you know). That alone provides competitive advantage, so it could also be a compelling reason for them to buy exclusively from our particular client/Blackberry wholesaler.

See how this works? Not only have you defined a very specific *audience* — you've also defined a very specific *experience* that is meaningful to that audience in some way. Something that fulfills a **critical need**; something important enough to motivate *use*.

3. **How is our product going to be different from (direct and indirect) competitors?** Bob's Blackberry Barn has been the distributor of choice for more than 70% of our user base. So it's going to be tough to unseat him as king of this particular hill. What can we do that Bob can't? Is our new real-time tracking feature enough to convince his customers to work with us instead? Are we at least **on par** with everything else he offers?

And it's not just about direct competitors like Bob. You also have to consider **indirect competition** as well. Things your audience might go for instead of what you're offering, because it's **close enough**.

What about *Raspberry* wholesalers, for example? Sure, it's a different fruit, but it's less expensive and CNN just did a story on how the National Raspberry Association is making a big pitch to the baking industry right now. What incentives are they offering these chefs that might make them order Raspberries instead of Blackberries?

These are questions that, while seemingly tangential, absolutely do impact your feature set and your design decisions. As such, they have to be asked.

The High Cost of Misunderstanding

This may all seem painfully obvious, but you'd be surprised (or not, for those of you who have some experience) at how often a project dives right into design and development at word *GO!* without covering any of this.

Unless you know, to some reasonable degree, what value you're giving people, and why it matters specifically to *them*, you're shooting in the dark. You're hoping that you hit something. And that's not a good place to be, even if the end product isn't yours.

Because inevitably, when the project finishes and the rubber hits the road, **you're still on the hook** for its success. And that particular song goes like this:

⇒ When the mobile app launches and the real-time tracking *isn't included* because you didn't want to be bothered asking questions or interviewing users, the chefs **don't use it**.

→ And when the mobile app isn't used, the client begins to wonder **why they paid you all this money** to redesign it.

→ And when the client begins to wonder about such things, **she gets aggravated**.

→ And when she gets aggravated, she starts **pointing fingers**.

→ And when she starts pointing fingers, I guarantee that **one of them will be pointed squarely at you**.

Obviously, this is *not* a place you want to be.

Every project, of any kind, involves any number of different people. And as we've established, they all have different roles, motivations and goals related to the work at hand.

From the client stakeholders with their project team, to your project team, to end-users, every person has very specific ideas in his mind about what this thing is going to do, along with how it's going to look and act.

So unless the scenario above appeals to you, take great pains to make sure everyone involved has a **shared understanding** of what those ideas are.

CHAPTER 5

Turning Strategy Into Scope

OMMISSIONS REPORTING - SCENARIO Ⓐ

```
☺ → ( LOG IN ) → [ HOME ] → [ COMMISSIONS ] → ( ENTER PIN )
```

```
( HOME AGAIN ) → [ COMMISSIONS ] → [ COMMISSIONS SUMMARY ] → ( SCROLL FO DEPOSIT AMT. )
```

```
[ YOUR BIZ / COMMISSION REPORTS ] → ( CHOOSE DATE ) → ( DOWNLOAD REPORT ) → ( OPEN IN MS EXC )
```

```
( REFORMAT .XLS TO BE PRINT-FORMAT ) → ( PRINT )
```

COMMISSIONS REPORTING - SCENARIO Ⓑ

```
☺ — ( LOG IN ) → [ BIZ MGMT / COMMISSION SUMMARY ] → ( SELECT AGENT # (DROPDOWN) )
```

```
[ COMMISSION REPORT PREVIEW ] → ( SCROLL DOWN FOR "DETAIL" TABLE ) → ( PRINT )
```

RODUCTION +
COMMISSION)

Have you ever worked on a project where new feature requests seemed endless? A situation where you are knee deep into development: you're past alpha, *way* past beta. You're into final programming and QA testing and putting what you think are the final touches on the site, or the app, and the client calls and says:

> *"I was thinking* (Red Alert!! Red Alert!!)...*what if a customer purchases something that isn't really included in their current service contract? What if they want A, B or C, but we don't support those options in the current contract?"*

To which you say, as calmly and as respectfully as is humanly possible, *"I have no idea what you're talking about."*

To which they explain that while these options are *available* on the site for purchase, a customer's particular service contract may make them *ineligible* to do so. So what if they purchase them and pay us, even though they shouldn't be able to do that?

And you're thinking to yourself... **why in God's name did I not know about this six months ago?**

Avoiding the Neverending Project

It's pretty much common knowledge, or it should be, that the discovery of requirements during UI design, or during development, is pretty much a recipe for disaster. Unfortunately, it happens quite often, which is one of the reasons office buildings don't have windows that open.

But no matter how much we all believe this is bad, no matter how hard we work to avoid this situation, it still happens. Most of us have come to terms with the fact that it's natural for clients to remember some infrequently used feature or edge case once they actually *see something* on the screen.

That's because not everyone has the same capacity for abstract thinking. For many people, once something is **visible**, it's more **real**. So in many ways, seeing a wireframe or an actual UI provides a needed foundation for analysis.

That's why a client, while reviewing a UI design, will often say *"Ohhhhhhh, you know what? We can't do that because of A, B, C, and/or D."* And that will lead you to a great moment of self-righteous anger, during which you will blame them for not having their requirements properly defined or clearly communicated. At that point you will feel like a victim — which feels great because hey, it's someone else's fault.

Except... it isn't.

This is **our problem**, not theirs.

And quite often, the reason it's our problem is because a lot of us tend to rush into the design and development process **without really, fully understanding everything that our solution needs to do**. We didn't take the time to properly define scope. Or, as is more often the case, we didn't raise the red flag when we *knew* scope wasn't properly defined and the client gave the green light to move forward.

As I mentioned earlier, silence is almost always interpreted as *agreement* — and that can get you in trouble.

In order to be successful, you have to hold yourself fully accountable for making sure scope is clearly defined. You have to take the attitude that if you don't do it, no one will. Whether that's true or not is irrelevant. Unless you take a proactive lead in defining scope, you're in for a world of pain. Trust me on this one.

Whether you're using a Lean or Agile methodology, or some related iterative process, you *still* have to properly define scope. You still need to make sure everybody involved shares a common understanding of what you are all building and how that relates to the project's overall goals and user needs.

You want to be sure everyone agrees on what you're doing and why. This gives you a **benchmark** to evaluate the progress of the project. At any given stage you have a clear view of what you've all done thus far (and how well you've done it), and you have a pretty solid sense of what you might expect in the future.

All that said, no scope is air-tight final. Don't expect to define scope to the degree where you can say ***"Beyond the shadow of a doubt, this is exactly what it's going to be and we will not deviate no matter what!!"*** Sorry, not possible. New things are going to come to light as the project progresses.

However, if you've done the work up front to clearly define your scope — if you've clearly defined the boundaries of what you can and *cannot* do, what you are and are *not* going to do — life gets a *lot* easier.

Scope Tradeoffs

Among the features and functions that you've decided are (a) important and (b) included, you'll have to make a tradeoff (or several) between three key things that factor into any project: **time**, **quality** and **cost**.

We've all heard the old joke where the client says, *"I want my project to be done **fast**, **good**, and **cheap**."* And the hired gun looks back at them and says, "Okay, **pick two**." Here's a slightly modified version that explains the reality of the situation a little more clearly. Multiple versions of this litter the Internet and I have not been able to track down the original author, but it's too good not to share here. So with apologies:

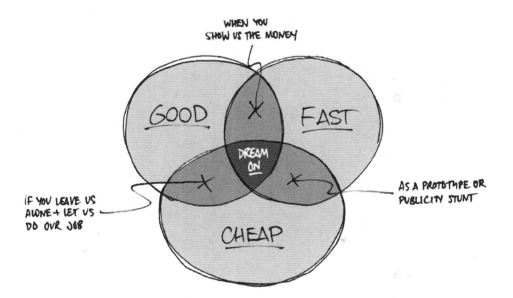

Now this is just a little humor to make a point; it's never a good idea to be rude to a potential client, or to *anyone* for that matter. But when you're defining what's included and what's not, you have to remember that even a *small change* in your defined plan will automatically result in at least one (if not all) of the following:

1. More **time** will be needed

2. More **money** will be needed

3. **Quality** will either increase or decrease

All of which, of course, place a strain on your available resources and your ability to succeed. Defining and managing project scope is all about making sure you consider, understand and manage those tradeoffs.

In the next few sections, I'm going to shed some light on exactly how you do that. And if nothing else, you'll walk away with a solid sense of how to tell when scope isn't properly defined. This will serve as your beacon, your signal to take a step back and say *"Waaaaaait a minute, we're not done here; there are things we don't know yet. And until we know how deep the water is, no one's diving in."*

Avoiding Perpetual Beta

The first reason we define scope is to get the train on the tracks, and to get everybody moving and doing the work of strategizing, designing and developing. We're working to avoid the curse of **perpetual beta**, which I have no doubt many of you are familiar with. There are any number of things that can trip up progress, and in my experience, taking the time to properly define scope negates the majority of them.

When you define scope, you're essentially forcing everybody (albeit politely) to see and address any potential conflicts:

- ➡ **What are the inherent risks related to what we're doing?** What haven't we considered yet? Who haven't we talked to?

- ➡ **Do we have a clear picture of indented outcomes at specific points between start and finish?** Are they clearly defined and achievable?

⇒ **Where is it possible that we'll get stuck?** What limitations on time, money or talent exist?

Asking those kinds of questions, and really thinking hard about the answers, goes a long way in making sure that the time you invest in designing and building is well spent. A clearly defined scope makes everyone more **productive**, more **proficient** and a LOT less stressed. And the client is a lot less stressed too, because they see clear progress. So the time and effort you devote up front to defining scope will serve you well later on.

The reason we *document* the established scope is to give the entire team, on your side and on the client side, a **reference point** for progress during the project lifecycle. A clear scope also gives you a common way to talk about those things in a manner that everybody is going to understand — because you all call it the same thing. You don't have to write a novel; just capture it somewhere, somehow and make sure every person involved has access to it.

Let's walk through a quick scenario: You have multiple registration processes. There's a registration for **end-customers**, but there are additional, distinct registration processes for **distributors** and **manufacturers**. And there's yet *another* registration process for **advertisers**.

All these folks will need to use different parts of what you're building, and each of those parts will ask for different criteria to determine customer eligibility or service levels.

Now assume we're having a conversation, and somebody says *"Oh, that happens during the **registration process**."*

Uh...*which* registration process are we talking about?

Is it the **client** registration process?

The **manufacturer** registration process?

The **advertiser** registration process?

Laugh if you will, but these conversations are absolutely no fun whatsoever, and I've had more of them than I can possibly count. By simply being specific — by documenting the fact that from now on, we're going to call this the **client registration process** and it consists of **this data** and **these steps** — everybody knows what we're talking about.

And for anyone who doesn't know, that decision is documented and shared, which means that, at any time, they can pull up that document and get educated. That sure beats waiting a week for schedules to open up so a meeting that doesn't really need to happen can be scheduled.

The rise of UX, design and development processes such as Lean, or Agile, or any of these methodologies, discourages lengthy documentation, a practice I agree with. When these processes are misunderstood, however, people get the mistaken idea that **no documentation of *any kind*** is necessary. But that approach isn't true to Lean or Agile practice — it's more like the proverbial throwing out the baby with the bathwater.

In the two-plus decades I have been doing this, eliminating documentation only results in one thing: a product with a slew of features, each of which has remained incomplete for the *last four months*. Every iteration has profoundly failed to match both the original idea for the feature, along with the team and client's collective expectation of what it is and how it's supposed to work.

Sure, we're iterating — we're constantly putting stuff out and reviewing, tweaking and improving it — but nobody fully understands what it is they're building. No one knows what those parts and pieces are *really* called or how they're all supposed to work together. So we're working. And re-working. And re-working. We're running fast, no doubt about it — but we're doing it on a *treadmill*.

Indulge me for a minute and let me explain why writing things down — documenting them somewhere in some small detail — matters. And why doing so has a *profound* impact on user and customer experience:

Have you ever been to a restaurant where the waiter memorizes your order instead of writing it down? I have, and *I absolutely, positively* **hate** *that*. Know why? Because unless I'm sitting in a five-star establishment, he is going to get my order *wrong*.

At least eight times out of ten.

And if there are a dozen people with me, he's going to get a few more wrong as well. And you know what? I'm not impressed even one iota that you are able to remember all of this in your brain. Especially since cognitive psychology and basic physiology proves that you *can't* actually do so in the first place.

What *really* impresses me? What makes me *truly* happy and provides a deeply meaningful, satisfying experience? **Get my order right**. The first time.

Unless there is a common reference point that everybody can refer to as each iteration occurs, you will live in the land of perpetual beta. Case CLOSED. No one will ever convince me that no documentation is a good idea. No documentation essentially means no *win*. I'm here to tell you that if nothing is documented, your project will quickly turn into a giant snowball, gaining size and speed as it rolls ever faster downhill.

And you, my friend, are standing at the bottom of said hill.

Again, this doesn't mean you have to write a novel. It doesn't have to be "formal" in any sense of the word. But you do have to write down all the **essential features**, **components**, and **functions**. I don't believe in specification documents either — nobody reads them, and that's the truth. Agile practitioners are completely correct when they say a two hundred page requirements document is outdated the minute it's complete. I totally agree with that.

But writing *nothing* down is every bit as short-sighted.

A common understanding of features, schedules, and milestones puts the end squarely in sight. It puts everybody on the same page, it gives everybody a common reference point, and a shared understanding of **what we're after** and **how we're going to get there**.

No matter what your process is, you *must* do this.

Know What You're Building (and What You're *Not*)

During the initial stages of any project, everybody has ideas about features. Your team, the client's team, end users, customers, the CEO's brother-in-law's cousin. The point is everybody is going to suggest stuff. All these ideas are going to come out of the air, and some of them will be very interesting, useful and in some cases very valid suggestions.

But more than a few of those things that sound like good ideas simply may not be **possible**. At least not **right now**, anyway.

We may not have the time or the budget or the talent to pull these things off. So, although this is certainly the time for idea generation and brainstorming, it's also critically important to draw a clear line between what's doable *right now* versus what has to wait for later.

Engineers I've known are fond of saying *"Anything can be done. The question is how long it's going to take to do it."* When you don't know the answer to the "how long" part of that question, you have to keep a running list that you must pay close attention to. You have to **qualify** the things on it to the best of your ability.

Maybe it's written on a whiteboard with a big DO NOT ERASE in red at the top. And maybe it looks a little something like this:

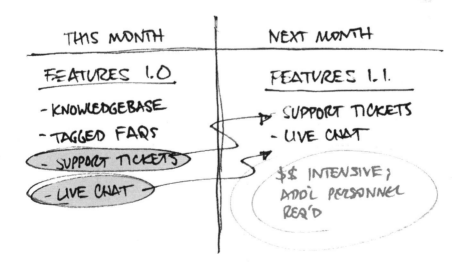

Maybe three weeks ago this all seemed feasible, but right now something has to wait. That dynamic support ticket system and live chat feature are too expensive for the budget. And by the way, we don't currently have the bandwidth to devote time to those features. And let's not even mention the fact that HR hasn't started hiring people to work tickets and chat with customers!

As such, we relegate those three things to the **next iteration**, next month. We'll revisit them then, see if they still make sense and figure out what's possible.

It's a simple matter of managing **what** you're doing and **when** you're going to do it. Again, the key is to *write it down in the first place*. If you don't have the list, it's pretty damn hard to make those decisions. And if you're making decisions without the list, **you're guessing**.

You may *think* you know what has to get done this month, but you're kidding yourself. You don't. And it's through no shortcoming of your own — that spongy mass between your ears simply isn't capable of that degree of perfection.

No matter how great your talents, you simply cannot keep all that stuff in your head. You cannot expect to charge through and have a solid, continued, miraculously updated sense of what's going to fit in, and what's not. There are roughly 80,000 miles of research to bear this out, by the way (*see the **Resources** section at the end of the book*). So please understand that this is not just *Joe's opinion on how things work* (even if I do happen to be more opinionated than your average stadium full of people).

So once again: **document it**. Whether that means a snippet of information delivered on a project management site, trading emails back and forth or writing something on a whiteboard and leaving it up there for everybody to see it, the important thing is that you **do it**.

It doesn't matter what form it takes, or how long, or how formal. What matters is that you write it down so, at any given moment, everyone knows:

⇒ **What** we're doing

⇒ **When** we're doing it

⇒ What we're **not** doing

⇒ What we're not doing **right now**.

Scope Creep: Just Say No

One of the biggest reasons to define scope is to avoid what's called *Scope Creep*. Scope Creep happens when additional features, additional suggestions and ideas for functionality not only keep coming up, but they also become *promises*. Promises that are now assumed to be included in the final product.

This usually means that someone on your team has the **"sure, we can do that" disease**. Whether it's someone actually on the design or development team, a Project Manager who's far removed from reality or an Account Representative too eager to say yes, someone's not guarding the gate.

A friend of mine likes to call it a *"death by a thousand cuts."* Each little addition, each little feature doesn't seem like much in and of itself. But collectively, their impact is **enormous**.

Every time that seemingly harmless little snowball rolls forward, it gets an inch bigger.

Every time someone says *"That will probably take me a day to do, so it's no big deal,"* that snowball gets bigger.

Every time the Project Manager says *"Guys, we have to do this to keep the client happy,"* that snowball gets bigger.

Every time something not already in the specs — and therefore unaccounted for — is agreed upon, **the snowball grows exponentially**. It gets bigger and faster and stronger and increasingly harder to *stop*.

Before you know it, that snowball-turned-avalanche is obliterating everything in its path — deadlines, budget estimates and the sanity of everyone involved. The inevitable crash is coming.

Scope creep kills project success, efficiency and profitability faster than anything I know. The customer wonders why can't get the work done that you agreed to. And you and you and your team are frustrated and can't see how any of this can even be accomplished — *and who the hell agreed to this anyway??*

All that hindsight is really, *really* painful. And it can be avoided.

Just say no — or, at least, not right *now*.

Capisce?

Strategic Tradeoffs and Product Evolution

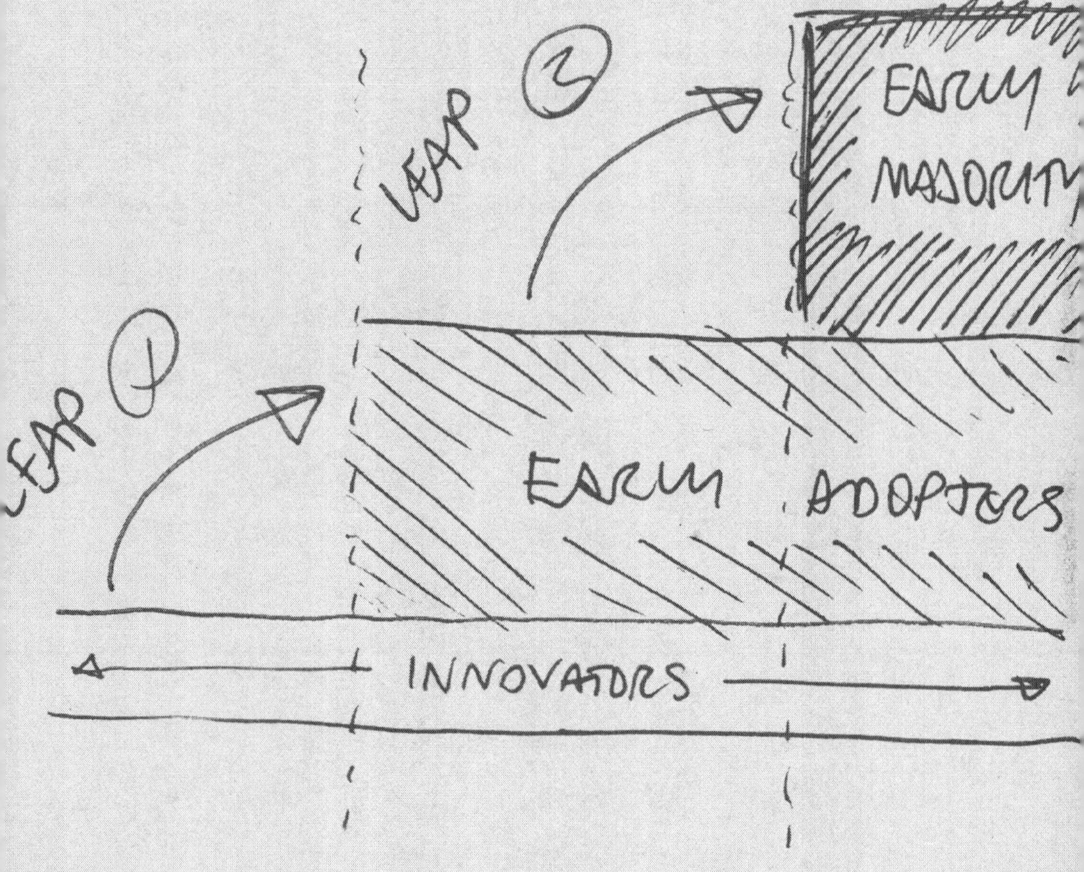

LEAP ①
LEAP ②
EARLY MAJORITY
EARLY ADOPTERS
INNOVATORS

Every choice you make in life almost always means that you'll have to give up something else, somewhere else. It's no different in the world of product development. Just like many of our strategic decisions, **tradeoffs** are an essential part of scoping a product. From what you decide to offer to how much of it you will design or build at any given moment, you are making tradeoffs.

Every feature or function you design — or intend to build — will absolutely affect a number of factors tied to success:

⇒ Making sure the **strategic objectives** of the product become reality via UX, design, features and functionality

⇒ The degree of **value** the finished product delivers to **customers**

⇒ The degree of **value** the finished product delivers to **end users** (not always the same as customers)

⇒ The degree of **value** the finished product delivers to the **business** (meaning return on their investment)

⇒ The team's ability to meet established **sprint** or **launch deadlines**

⇒ Staying within the established **project budget**

⇒ The team's ability to properly **design, implement, integrate** and **support** all required and/or requested **functionality**

A gentleman by the name of Michael Porter wrote the book — both figuratively and literally — on competitive strategy. In a widely-cited piece for the *Harvard Business Review*, titled *What Is Strategy?* he explains two crucial reason why tradeoffs are so very essential to business strategy:

1. Tradeoffs **create the need** for **choice**.
2. Tradeoffs **purposefully limit** what's offered.

Pay attention to the two most important words there: "**purposefully limit**." These aren't *deficiencies*; we're not talking about things that are lacking or missing in some way. What Porter is talking about are thoughtful, purposeful decisions to *limit* a feature set — in order to focus on delivering what matters most.

In other words, Porter is advocating for **Constraints**. And constraints are very different from **limitations**. Let's talk for a minute about the difference between the two.

Both constraints and limitations are boundaries. But they're not the same *kind* of boundary. A limit defines what's *possible*; a constraint defines what's *appropriate*. Here's what I mean:

⟹ If someone tells you that the new web portal
  must be coded using .NET and only .NET,
  that's a **limitation**.

⟹ If that same person tells you the platform is
  your choice, as long as it supports a user-
  friendly Content Management System (CMS),
  that's a **constraint**.

Simply put, a constraint *frames context*. It's a guide that shows you how to strategize and design within the context of what's appropriate. Constraints are often seen as limits, but they are really an **invitation to innovate**. Tradeoffs that make *smart strategic sense* are born from constraints; they are *purposefully* designed into the process.

Tradeoff Case Study: IKEA

In his article, Michael Porter makes an example of the blue and yellow behemoth who brought modern design to every bachelor pad in America: IKEA. Why? Because IKEA has built a successful business model on some very purposeful tradeoffs, born from very purposeful constraints, producing very positive results for both the company and its customers.

IKEA *owns* the value loop like very few organizations can, and that has allowed them to focus on the most valuable part of their business: their customers. By way of example, here are three of IKEA's strategic tradeoffs:

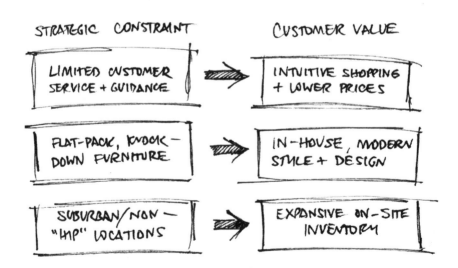

Let's look at each of those tradeoffs in more detail:

1. **IKEA limits customer service, but delivers intuitive shopping and low prices.** When you go into the store, there aren't a lot of employees to guide or assist you. It's a very DIY experience. You walk through the store, you write down what you want, and then you go pick it out yourself.

   By the numbers, fewer employees in the store is smart: it lowers their overhead. That lowered overhead means they can charge less for their products, which obviously benefits customers. And, because they're asking customers to pick out their own stuff, they realize the shopping experience has to be that much more simple, intuitive and easy. They have purposefully designed it to be so: everything has a numeric code attached to it. All you do is write down the code, and then find it in the aisles. The signage is clear and the wayfinding is simple.

2. **IKEA doesn't carry anything that comes pre-assembled.** IKEA has what is known as flat-pack or knock-down furniture. But again, it's a purposeful tradeoff: they've given up pre-assembled stuff, and they've given up doing the assembly as well. Because the company doesn't bear the cost of assembling the product — and a host of other costs associated with personnel, equipment, electricity, etc. — prices can remain low and consistent.

   Every IKEA product is warehoused right in the store; it doesn't have to be sourced from anywhere, so its always available. And since the products have a very modern style, this constraint has enabled IKEA products to be just what they are. Whether flat-pack or knock-down, they answer a customer desire: well-designed, functional, cool furniture at affordable prices.

3. **IKEA stores are located in suburban locations.** Their stores aren't located downtown or in the hip/ trendy neighborhood heart of things. The locations they choose allow them to provide a huge on-site inventory. Everything is at your fingertips as a customer: it's all there. You don't have to go anywhere else because the store itself is the warehouse.

These are all very purposeful tradeoffs, born from a clear understanding of what the business needs, what people want and what's *possible*. IKEA has given up things in some areas to realize gains in others. All the while making sure those decisions equal *better value* for customers.

Scoping a project, determining feature set and priority, is no different. You have to make the same kinds of strategic tradeoffs described here. You have to figure out what you and customers need to **gain**, and think hard about what you have to **give up** in order to realize those gains. And then, of course, you have to determine whether the result is worth the sacrifice.

Product Evolution: the *Long Wow*

Approaching project scope from a strategic standpoint also means defining product evolution:

→ How will the product **change, evolve** and **grow** over time?

→ How do we make sure it remains **relevant** to people?

In UX & marketing circles, what needs to happen is referred to as the **Long Wow**. To my knowledge, the term was first coined in 2007 by Brandon Schauer, now CEO of Adaptive Path. In an article titled (what else) *The Long Wow*, he explains:

> *"The process is a means to achieving long-term customer loyalty through systematically impressing your customers again and again. Going a step beyond just measuring loyalty, the Long Wow is an experience-centric approach to fostering and creating it."*

Essentially, as the product is used more and more over time, the Long Wow should provide new experiences, recurring delight, recurring surprise and recurring ***"WOW, I didn't know it could do that!"***

This isn't a set-it-and-forget-it proposition; it's a *continual evolution*. It means additions, modifications and the relentless quest for improvement. In the world of software, sites and systems, we're all familiar with the concept of progressive releases with new or improved features. The software, systems and apps we use are constantly updated (whether we want it or not).

The Long Wow transcends digital, however: **it's a cycle of increasing expectation that's embedded in *everything* that we humans do**. We expect progressive, continuous value over the life of just about everything that we use.

And, with the proliferation of mobile devices at our beck and call, that level of expectation has grown exponentially. Most of us have very little tolerance for things that don't meet our expectations, because we know there are infinite alternatives at our fingertips.

Here's a quick example of how a strategic misstep in the release cycle can cause users and customers to abandon a product.

Pick any app on your mobile phone, and you'll find that there's an **interaction pattern** for how an item is deleted. There's a flow of actions and results that you've become used to, that you expect, when you want to delete something. A dialog window for example, appears consistently with the same message, the same standard buttons and labels, e.g. DELETE.

The **first time** you saw the pattern, you had to learn it. All you do now, however, is *do it*. Habit and reflex have taken over; no conscious thought required. That's because you already *know* the pattern. It's always in the same place, the controls look the same every time and respond to your actions in the same way. Tap, tap, *done*.

And if other apps on your phone follow the same pattern, your efficiency increases. The pattern is the same even though it's a different app, so **you don't have to stop and think**.

But when a new upgrade comes out and the pattern changes, or other new apps use a **completely different pattern**, it all grinds to a halt.

You have to start over.

The speed and dexterity gained is gone, because you now have to stop and examine the new pattern and think, *"Am I doing this correctly?"*

The more variance in the established pattern, the more work your brain has to do... *just to figure out what to do.* The brain is good at recognizing that something's different from what it already knows, even if it can't specifically identify the difference.

The point here is that *any difference*, visual or otherwise, forces the brain to **re-evaluate** how the pattern works.

This is enough to motivate someone to start looking for another app that works the way they expect it to. And when that happens, loyalty — and customers — are lost.

When interactions and outcomes become consistent (and predictable), people only have to learn the controls and patterns once — and then employ them without much active thinking. This allows them to concentrate on the **task at hand**.

Which, if you think about it, is the primary reason they're using your product in the first place :-)

Anatomy of a Long Wow Experience

Part of planning a Long Wow experience means thinking through your incremental releases and updates. Not just **what** you're going to change, but **why** you're going to change it, and how much **value** will be derived from that change. And, like the preceding example, you also want to think through any possible disruption you might introduce — and whether the value gained is worth pissing a few people off. Strategic tradeoffs, remember?

The goal then, with product design of any kind, is to systematically serve and impress customers — again, again, and again. We're trying to create a succession of successes, all of which lead to an increasing sense of accomplishment or achievement.

Nowhere is this approach applied or proven more consistently than in the world of smartphone apps and games. Let's talk a little about how the Long Wow creates successful products in that realm.

Motivation and Mastery

The Long Wow in an apps — particularly a gaming app — comes from **mastery**, which is linked to **motivation**. Gaming apps in particular put a user on the motivating path of mastery — beat the next level, find the hidden bonuses, explore entirely new worlds and scenarios.

Daniel Pink's *Drive* pointed out that **intrinsic motivation** – the joys that are a natural part of an activity – matters more to us than external factors, e.g. do this to get my boss (or doctor or girlfriend or wife) off my back. And while short-term motivation can spur a download or a purchase (*"learn this software if you want to keep your job"*), it fades away just as quickly.

For passionate users, the intrinsic motivation that drives them doesn't come from learning to do something, or making something they already do easier. It's also not about saving money via special deals or coupons or contests.

Instead, what matters most to the majority of app users is **growing their competence**. Getting progressively *better* at something. The experience they're after is a deft balance of what they do well and what they want to do better.

And lest we forget about the business end of UX, the experience also has to integrate what we (or the client) wants the user to do. That balancing act looks something like this:

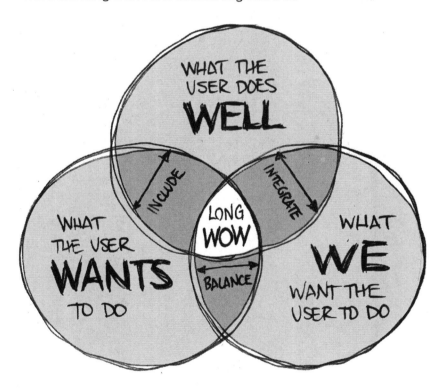

Adapted from *The "What" and "Why" of Goal Pursuits: Human Needs and the Self-Determination of Behavior*, Edward L. Deci & Richard M. Ryan, 2009

In her excellent book *Badass: Making Users Awesome*, Kathy Sierra does a great job explaining why that intrinsic motivation is the key to long-term product success. And although she doesn't use the term Long Wow, that is most definitely what she's talking about. Companies, in Kathy's opinion, focus too much on the tool, and not enough on **how the tool helps users advance their skills** (and themselves). In other words, they don't spend nearly enough time on context of use.

A camera, for example, is a tool. *Becoming a better photographer*, however, is the larger contextual goal — and the key to lasting motivation.

A camera app with a lot of features is great, and may be initially attractive. But if that same app actually helps the user to become better at photography, continually increasing their knowledge or competence or ability over the life of using the app, you've got a loyal user (and repeat customer).

Repeated, Recognized Reward

So the Long Wow, in this case, is making sure that a continuous, evolving system of **repeated reward** is designed into the experience. Reward that's internalized and felt and acknowledged by the person using the product. Otherwise, popularity fades.

Angry Birds, for example, took the gaming world by storm and was one of the most successful apps in history. But the fanfare died down just as quickly when new releases of the game failed to deliver anything new and remarkable to users. Subsequent editions didn't offer any new challenges, new ways to increase skills, new opportunities for mastery.

Once mastery is achieved, the brain is looking for the next challenge. It's the same reason bright students often perform poorly in classes that don't challenge their intellect: their perception is that there's nothing to be learned that they don't already know. When challenges appear in the context of increasing mastery, people stick around. If it's too easy, doesn't move them closer to a goal or doesn't deliver the desired result, they start looking for something new.

Take a look at the iTunes app store or Google Play and you'll find that the majority of apps are designed to **reward continuous use**. For health and wellness apps, continued use over time delivers real, tangible benefits that are physically experienced. Productivity apps deliver repeated value with use by helping someone become more organized, more productive, or maybe just a little less forgetful. Creative apps allow people to develop creative talents in a context they're already physically and emotionally connected to (smartphone/tablet use).

And the result of action taken in the context of motivation is *fun*.

What "Fun" Really Means

This intrinsic motivation we're talking about is also what makes using well-designed apps or games fun. Game designer Raph Koster wrote a seminal article called *An Atomic Theory of Fun Game Design*, in which he essentially says that fun from games is tied to the idea of mastery. From solving puzzles to avoiding challenging obstacles to shooting zombies, games provide challenges that produce feelings of accomplishment. Of progress. Of increasing mastery.

Make all of this happen continuously over time with each release, and guess what? You've designed a Long Wow experience.

Motivation isn't magic; it's a purposeful component of strategic UX design. It's something you should be thinking about from the moment you have an idea for a product, from the moment the client says *"we need to…"* The Long Wow of intrinsic motivation comes from taking the time to figure out how interactions, feedback and new options or features can walk hand-in-hand with the user's underlying goal of getting *better* at something.

Any and all variety in flow, interaction or functionality in each new release should serve the goal of delivering a continual sense of achievement. Everything else is secondary.

Planning a Long Wow Experience

Brandon Schauer's article posited **four basic steps** to creating a Long Wow experience, and they hold absolutely true nearly a decade later. It looks like this:

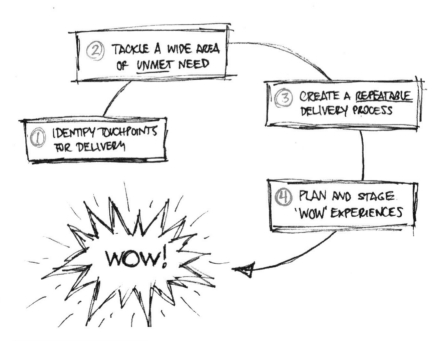

Here's how it works:

1. **Identify touchpoints for delivery.**

   The first thing you have to do is identify how to deliver your experiences. To who? Where? What experiences can or should be combined to deliver that WOW in the context of achievement?

   Start by selecting a small set of touchpoints across channels that can be (1) *coordinated* to meet a specific need, and (2) *remixed* in a way to deliver new solutions as you come up with them. Wearables like the Fitbit, for example, utilize three touchpoints:

   ⇒ The wearable **device** itself.

   ⇒ The **smartphone** you pair it with.

   ⇒ The **website** you use to manage both.

   Fitbit chose these touchpoints to deliver three ways for you to interact with the product. Because of this multi-faceted approach, the experience of using the device transcends any **single event**. Fitbit started by asking the essential questions: How (and how often) are we going to engage people? What are the points of contact and interaction? These are the touchpoints you need to think about as you design.

2. **Tackle a wide area of unmet need.**

   Next, you have to find where the customer experience is lacking. What things have been overlooked? Where is the greatest potential to discover or deliver something truly new? Here's a hint: this will typically be something that you're **passionate** about. And it's also something that you should have some kind of competitive advantage with — meaning you understand it or can deliver it better than anyone else.

Your chosen area should be something that you feel like you can return to **repeatedly** to keep adding new insight, new features and new experiences. It should be a space where there is abundant opportunity for motivation and mastery. It may be an opportunity to identify an altogether new space, or it may be an opportunity to **reinvent an old space** that everyone else is neglecting.

3. **Create a repeatable delivery process.**
   The third step is developing the ability to repeat the WOW on a continuous, **consistent** basis. Start with the strengths you already have, which may be a simple matter of cost versus benefit. Or superior product quality. Or a very thorough understanding of what motivates your audience.

   You take those things and blend them with research, prototyping, product design, and/or interactive design. You focus on those experiences that give you a clear idea of what's *possible* and *achievable*. What's important is that your focus remains on the **impact** of the experiences over time. What will people gain competence with over time? How will fresh, meaningful challenges be designed, implemented and sustained?

Keep your focus here, as opposed to the tool itself; usability of the interface or the physical design of the device. It's all about the experience, about how each update makes people **feel**: are they getting the WOW, the *newness*, the sense of accomplishment, with each release?

Creating and evolving a repeatable process means you have to know — and be able to *show* — how the experience brings something **meaningful** and **motivating** to the user's life. It has to be painfully clear where the WOW happens and how you're going to make sure it keeps happening.

4. Plan and stage your wow experiences.

Understand that you're not going to be able to develop all of your ideas at once. In fact, there's a lot of inherent risk in attempting to do so — because for starters, it's extremely difficult to do. None of us can accurately predict the future, so purposeful, incremental iteration is the key to figuring out what works and what's realistic.

You need to plan the **intervals** between releases appropriately, so you have time to measure user reaction. Watch how people use what you've given them. Pay attention to what they tell you is underperforming or missing altogether. People might tell you what's good, but they'll *definitely* tell you what's bad. And while the bad is always harder to hear, it's where the most valuable information, insight and understanding come to light.

Your task at this point? Organize a **pipeline of possible WOW moments** that can be introduced through your touchpoints over the long haul. As you continue to learn more about your customers — how they perceive those WOW moments and what their larger goals are — both your pipeline *and* your ideas will change. They will evolve and develop further.

Doing the work now, outlining where and when those additional experiences will emerge in the future allows you to plan and coordinate the resources necessary to implement them.

You may not get it exactly right the first time, or even the third or fourth time, but you will be on a path that serves the greater goals that motivate people to use things.

A large part of delighting customers means introducing the right thing at the right time. As the saying goes, timing is everything.

But that's only half the story.

The other half is you. You, continuously working to test your assumptions and make sure that what you're giving people truly has **intrinsic value** that continues to build over time.

CHAPTER 7

Requirements: A Better Way

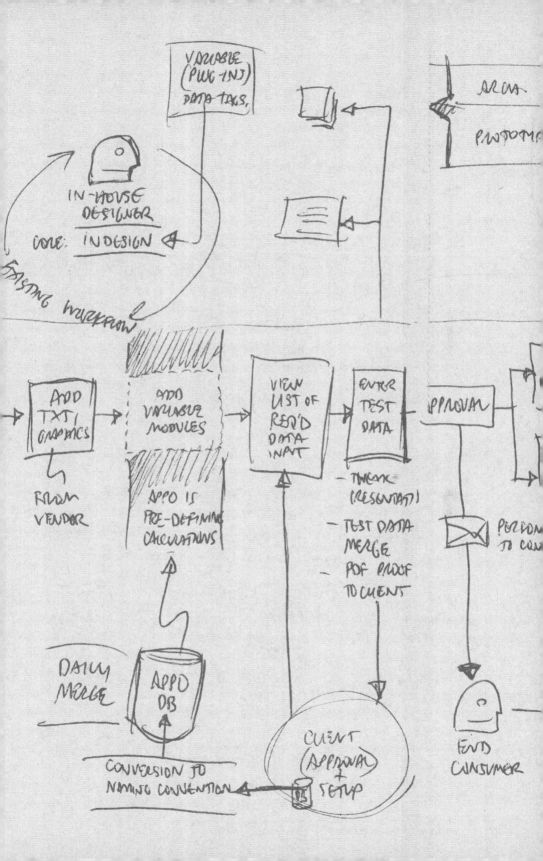

We started this journey by asking why we're doing any of this. Now it's time to ask *what*: What exactly are we going to do?

In terms of design and development, a product's feature set — what we've all agreed we're going to design and build — is defined by *functional requirements*.

The more complexity we have, the more requirements we need. The more features we decide to implement, the more specificity we need for how those features should be designed and implemented. In other words, there are more questions to be asked.

If your task is redesigning an existing product, your primary source of requirements will be the **people** that are using it now. For a new product, a target audience with specific needs that will be met by the new product will play that role. But remember the UX value loop: user experience isn't just about users.

Requirements and specifications will also come from the **stakeholders** we met earlier in this book. Not only do they (hopefully) know their business and what needs to be provided in order to satisfy their customers, they have a *big* stake in the outcome. They understand what needs to happen in order for the organization to get some return on their investment in the project.

So once again, you'll need to visit *both sides* of the value loop in order to determine requirements for features and functions. You'll use all the data, research and analysis you have thus far to begin generating requirements. And those requirements fall into three essential categories.

> ⇒ There are things people *say* they need.

> ⇒ Then there are things that they ***actually*** need.

⇒ And then finally, there are things that they *don't know* they need.

What People *Say* They Need

Ask any group of people what they want or need and you'll get no shortage of answers. Brainstorming sessions with concerned participants will result in a great number of new approaches and angles — and opinions will surface quickly.

Even in a "think big" situation where participants are encouraged to ignore all limitations, a lot of what comes up will be solid. You may very well decide to keep and implement several of the concepts discussed. But the majority of them will never make it past those initial sessions. That's normal, because not every idea is actually *possible*. You may not have the time, the technical expertise, the budget or the right people with the right skill sets to pull them off.

But you need to be hyper-critical of that first set of ideas. The reason, according to neuroscience expert Dr. Susan Weinshenk, is because we humans, no matter how smart or well-informed we may be, have a very common flaw:

We often make very confident — but equally *false* — predictions about our future behavior.

Imagining how you'd use something isn't the same as **actually** using it. And because the imagining part is easy, it's seductive to think that our perceptions of use are indeed reality. But it's just not true. Spend five minutes in a usability lab and I guarantee you will see, quite clearly, just how *enormous* the gap between perceived and actual use really is.

Without actual use, you're just speculating, *guessing* at how it might be used. The thorough understanding that only comes with repeated use is missing at this stage.

What's more, **our preferences are subject to our emotions**, which makes them a bit unstable and/or unreliable. How we feel about something is easily affected by the kind of day we're having. And we are certainly influenced by all of our experiences up to that point (related or not).

You know the old phrase *"don't knock it until you try it?"* The instability I'm describing is the reason that phrase exists.

The bottom line is that you don't really *know* if something is useful, valuable, relevant or positive until you actually **use it** and experience a **result** of that use.

In those initial "Think Big" sessions, you're really asking people to either **remember** past use or **speculate** on future use. Either way, there's no solid precedent specific to *this* set of tools, features, circumstances and possible outcomes. There's nothing to lean on other than a loosely educated guess about what *might* happen. So you must remember:

> **What people *say* they need isn't always what they *really* need.**

> **What people *say* they'll do isn't always what they *actually* do.**

So while you should absolutely consider all these generative ideas that come up in the beginning of a process, you should do so with more than a couple pounds of salt.

What People *Actually* Need

We've established that every idea expressed isn't necessarily a good idea. But while these things may not make into the final feature set, they can often be a stepping stone of sorts to the next level of features: things people actually need.

When we have trouble with something, imagining solutions to solve the problem is easy, almost effortless. Many of you will be familiar with the term "solution jumping," which is what happens when people start suggesting solutions before they're even sure what the problem is. We're good at it, so we do it often.

The problem with solution jumping is that it almost always addresses a **symptom** instead of the underlying problem. At the same time, that symptom is still the right place to start. Your task now is to *qualify* it, to play it forward and uncover the other actions, processes and motivations *attached* to it.

You may start out on a path that's a little wobbly, but that doesn't mean you're going to stay there. The way you get past the wobble is by investigating further:

⇒ Have we looked **beyond the tool** itself? Do we really understand what users expect to be able to do, how they need to be able to do it and why that matters to them?

⇒ Do we have any **evidence** that tells us this requirement solves a recurring problem that's affecting use or adoption?

⇒ Is there **research** we can lean on to provide insight? Or is there more we need to know about users, expectation and motivation?

It's both important and worthwhile to go through that exercise and to have those long drawn out discussions, no matter how pointless they can sometimes seem. Unless you go through the process of exploring all the parts related to what the user is doing, you'll never have a clear picture of what they (and the business) really need.

What People *Don't Know* They Need

One of my favorite quotes is from Harvard Marketing Professor Ted Lovett, which goes like this:

> *"People don't want quarter inch drills. They want quarter inch **holes**."*

Do you get that? What it means is that the **desired outcome**, what they're using the tool to do, is infinitely more important than the **chosen tool**.

When conversations are focused on clarifying what people expect the outcome to be — instead of a very narrow focus on features, functions, and product attributes — you're more likely to come up with better, more relevant solutions. You're more likely to uncover things that no one realized were a problem until now. You'll also likely discover that those things are causing at least a dozen other issues which, up until now, you thought were completely unrelated.

This isn't as easy as it sounds, mind you. Our natural tendency is to look at a mechanism for doing something first. Mainly because when problems arise, we look around for a way to get the job done *now*; we think about **convenience** first. That's human nature and it's hardwired in our brains.

So if I need to drill a quarter inch hole, I'm going to use **whatever does that easily and quickly**.

If I'm in the basement and my drill is in the garage upstairs, I may very well take the Phillips-head screwdriver in my pocket and poke a hole in the wall. Because it just happens to be about a quarter inch in diameter, and it's here with me. Convenience, in this case, trumps best practice.

Otherwise, I have to stop what I'm doing, walk upstairs, get the drill out of the cabinet, find a quarter-inch drill bit... which could be *anywhere* since I never put it back in the same place... insert the bit... punch a guide hole... you get the picture.

The bottom line is that we shouldn't be talking about the drill at all. Or its features. Or its functions. What we should be talking about is threefold:

1. The **problem** that people are facing

2. What their **desired outcome** is

3. What they're **most likely to do** to solve it — with or *without* your specific product!

Forget the product, forget the attributes, forget the specs. Focus on the *desired outcome* and the problem at hand.

Creating Useful Requirements with Use Scenarios

There are any number of formalized ways to go about generating requirements, and every discipline has it's own version. If you talk to IT folks, you'll get one story. If you talk to designers, you'll get another story, another process, and another stair-step list of things that have to be done. Agile folks have their own methodology for going about that.

But for my money, if you're looking for a really simple, bottom line way to figure out what the requirements need to be (and which matter most), you create what we call **use scenarios**.

The reason I *love* use scenarios and apply them religiously is because when people see something, they ask questions. The **visual conversation** fuels the verbal conversation. There are all sorts of *ancillary* things that can happen in a scenario — and in day-to-day reality — that don't necessarily get accounted for when we're strictly looking at form, feature, and function.

Over the past 26 years it's been my experience that without this process, those things are never surfaced, discussed or addressed. Which also means they're never agreed upon.

A use scenario is a short, simple narrative that describes how someone might go about trying to fulfill a specific need:

⟹ Sarah wants to save products to **different gift lists** for family members.

⟹ Bob needs to be able to compare **service rates**, **delivery options** and **support contract terms**.

⟹ Jill needs to be able to **add events** on the website to her **Outlook calendar**.

Whatever it may be, you start with the person doing the work. Define what their specific **role** is, what their specific **needs** are and what they're trying to **accomplish**. Use scenarios focus squarely on *context*, on real-world situations that people will find themselves in that relate to your particular product.

Here's an example of what my use scenarios look like:

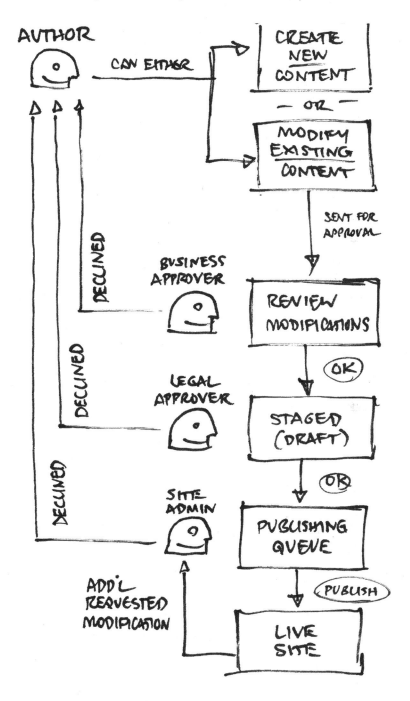

This use scenario came from a discussion about publishing workflow for a content management system. What I do in these situations is simply ask the client to **walk me through the process** verbally.

As they talk, I draw people, boxes, and arrows on a whiteboard (or on paper) that describe what happens. I'm going to walk you through this diagram and give you some examples of how something this simple can uncover important technical requirements.

The client says to me *"we'll have multiple **authors**, each of whom can either **create** new content, or **modify** existing content."* In return, I ask, *"Do the authors have access to all content, or only their own?"* The answer that comes back is *"well, they should only have access to their own content, but we're short-staffed, so there will be times when we'll need them to work on someone else's content."*

Several requirements that come from that simple exchange, which I also write on the whiteboard:

➡ System has to support multiple users (1 - N)

➡ Each user needs an individual system role and ID

➡ Default access should be restricted to content they create

➡ Need an admin role above them who can easily and quickly allow other authors to access their content

➡ Authors will likely need a WYSIWYG editor

→ Authors will need discrete action to submit content for approval

Then, they explain to me that once an author creates or modifies a piece of content, there are **two people who have to approve it** before it can be published.

First, a **business approver** in a specific department reviews the content. If it needs modification, she *declines* it, which means it goes back to the author who has to modify the existing content. If she *approves* the content, it goes further on down the chain to a legal approver, who can either decline or accept the content. If declined, it goes back to the author. If approved, it goes to the site admin, who is responsible for publishing it.

Here are the requirements that come from this exchange:

→ Two specific "approval" user roles (with unique ID) needed; second role only sees content if the first rejects it

→ Each "approval" user needs to receive notification that content is ready and requires their review and approval

→ Each "approval" user needs a way to view the content at various stages

→ Each "approval" user needs to be able to accept or reject the content

→ The next "approval" user in the chain should be automatically notified when content is approved (triggered notification) by the previous approver

- ⇒ "Site Admin" role with absolute publishing privileges is needed

- ⇒ "Site Admin" will need to be able to approve or reject content for technical reasons

- ⇒ Authors should be automatically notified as to whether content is approved or rejected (triggered notification)

I'm going to stop there, because I think our point is made. The client has only told me two very simple things thus far, and yet I have **more than a dozen requirements**. That's how this works. And that's how it *should* work; otherwise you're picking requirements out of the air, based on what you've done in the past or on what you believe should happen.

What's more, requirements don't just happen once: they can and should come from *every single conversation* you have with users and stakeholders.

Each one of the people in my diagram needs the ability to **see** information, and they need to be able to **act on it** in any number of ways. All it takes to figure that out is a very straightforward, simple conversation and someone like you drawing it out in the room with boxes and arrows.

Forget formal use cases, forget formal diagramming methodologies and rules. Just draw it out and label **who the players are** and **what they're doing**!

Page 129 shows another example of what a use scenario looks line. You'll notice that there is a core path of action and result, along with notes that describe what's happening, problems that occur and related questions.

It's not any more complicated than this. You draw, and you ask questions about each step, each decision point, each action:

→ What happens here?

→ What happens next?

→ What can the next person in the process *do* with what they have?

It's a very simple way of getting a baseline for what gets **created**, what gets **acted upon**, and how it all moves through any particular **process**. We're focusing on the people, we're focusing on the roles at hand and we're focusing on how they do what they do every day.

In a scenario, you're also considering what each person's **goals** are. For example, if you have someone who is approving all this content, one of their primary goals may be to know, at a single glance, what the status of any given piece of content is: who wrote it, where it is in the approval process, etc. They need the ability to keep all the details straight. Prioritize multiple reviews. They may need to create communications with other approvers, or with authors, to keep misunderstanding to a minimum.

Above all else, they may be praying for a tool that helps them **stay calm** in the face of angry authors and looming deadlines.

My point here is there are all sorts of **ancillary** things that can happen in a scenario — and in day-to-day reality — that don't necessarily get accounted for when we're strictly looking at form, feature, and function.

Always remember: use is all about human beings, and human beings are *complex*. There isn't always a straight line between

MUST-PASS RESULTS (SCREENSHOT)

└ QUICK VIEW OF ELEMENTS/PASSED OR FAIL

ELEMENT PASSED?

Y

N

RECOMM... (SCREENSH...

- REVIEWER RE ABLE... NON-COM... ELEMEN...
- CURRE... TO GO... TI GO IN...

GO TO THAT ELEMENT

ALERT ASC + OTHER PARTIES

* NO LINK TO ELEMENTS; REVIEWER HAS TO GO BACK NEW MENU

WHY NOT... THE ELEMENT...

REC'S SPECIF... W/ THAT EL...

"VIEW SURVEY" TOOL

SURVEY TOOL MAIN SCREEN

"NO IDEA HOW TO GET BACK"

GENER... "REV... RIVEN... VIE...

(MA... SA...

TAK... FOR...

TAKES USER COMPLETELY OUT OF CURRENT WORKFLOW!

TIONS

SUMMARIZED + DETAILED RESULTS

CLICK NAME OF CATEGORY

OS TO DIT T CTORS HAS EMENT

POSSIBLE POINTS VS. POINTS RECIEVED? WHERE ARE DEFICIENCIES?

MORE IMPORTANT THAN ANYTHING ELSE HERE!

60 TO ONY SEE Y ASSOCIATED T?

THIS SCREEN MAY BE EXTRANEOUS/ UNNECESSARY

EA. ELEMENTS
POINTS REC'D / POINTS POSSIBLE / % SCORE

(SCREENSHOT)

MOST VALUABLE INFO

REVIEWER FRIENDLY SURVEY TOOL

CIA)

OPENS IN NEW, SMALL WINDOW. HAVE TO CHANGE VIEW TO FULL SCREEN

CARLTON DOESN'T USE THIS— GOES TO "SURVEY UTILITIES"

TO "VIEW ALL EVALUATION COMMENTS"

SCREENSHOT NEEDS TO FOCUS IN THE COMMENTS — "MAJORITY OF MY WORK IS HERE" what we do and what we want to happen. As such, commit the following axiom of user-centered design to memory:

Task completion, in and of itself, does *not* equal success.

The only time a tool, workflow or process is successful is when it meets all the primary *and* ancillary needs of all the folks who are involved at every stage.

What About Use Cases and User Stories?

Kim Goodwin's *Designing for the Digital Age* does an excellent job of explaining why use cases and user stories don't provide much in the way of UX-focused requirements. So I will para-phrase her here.

Use cases and user stories, Goodwin says, don't consider or incorporate **how users *feel* about a feature or interaction**, nor do they investigate why a particular interaction or behavior provides a **better experience** for the user. Use cases and user stories focus on **roles** as opposed to personas: they design for *Jane the Bank Teller.*

In the use scenario work I just described, we're designing for *Jane the stressed-out bank teller who typically has a line of 10 impatient people at any given time and who desperately needs a way to navigate the system in half the time or automate com-plex, lengthy transaction sequences.*

Look Beyond Tasks and Activities

Good UX has to address a lot more than tasks and activities. For Jane, getting customers through the line and completing their transactions is **task completion**; she's already doing that now.

Doing this same task *better* — in a way that is more accurate, efficient and makes customers feel like the process was painless, pleasant and *really* fast — is **success**.

In our scenario a few pages back, the authors and approvers need to do the tactical things required of them, but they also want to be able to *keep track of it all* without losing their minds.

They want to know for sure that the next person in the chain has been notified so they don't have to badger them.

They want to be able to report status to their boss anytime s/he asks so they appear to be on top of things.

Those things, which fall *outside* the mechanical tasks of writing and reading content, are what constitute success.

"I want to look good to my boss" won't usually make it to most requirements lists, but it certainly *should*. Because if that doesn't happen, that person doesn't get what they need. And if they don't get what they need, neither does anyone else in the entire workflow. The system doesn't save the company the time or money they expected it to.

And that, my friends, is failure.

Making Use Scenarios Contextual with Personas

Remember the goofy little heads I drew in the diagram? Those are the people using what we're designing here, and as I think you know by now, your most critical task is to understand them. What they need to do, why they're motivated to do it and how they expect things to happen.

One of the ways you make this picture clearer is by creating a **persona** for each user.

There are plenty of prescriptions for persona creation, but they're all essentially the same: laundry lists that suggest it's possible to understand a person's motivation — and create an accurate, useful user persona — simply by checking boxes and asking questions related to behavior.

This is not that, because *that*, in my experience, doesn't *work*.

So instead, I'm going to give you a simple, practical process and two companion templates that will put you on the path to creating user personas that deliver real value to your design approach. I'm going to show you the best way I know to get a true understanding of a user that is formed by the messy realities of what it's like to be human.

There are two key steps in this process:

1. **First, you have to understand the person's context and develop empathy for them.** Empathy goes far beyond demographics, likes, dislikes, job roles and responsibilities. Empathy is about understanding the emotional drivers that affect the user's behavior, because **emotion will trump intellect** in almost every situation users find themselves in. Design for the emotion and you're truly designing for a person instead of a collection of possible attributes.

2. **Next, you have to uncover that person's behavioral attributes and motivations, in the context of multiple situations.** What has the person just

done or just finished doing when they encounter your product (site, app, tool)? What are they thinking and feeling at that moment, and how does that affect what they see and how they act? What **stress** is present in that situation, and how does it affect the person's perception and action?

Persona Creation Happens Immediately

I want to be clear that I explore both of the areas noted above *before* any face-time with users. *Before* I read any usage data the client has for me. *Before* I hear from stakeholders what people are having trouble with or are complaining about.

The minute you have any of that input, **your perception of who that user is** has been **irrevocably tainted**.

That's not your fault; it's how your brain is designed to work. Once you have those conversations, you will have predetermined ideas about what situations people find themselves in and what causes them to perceive things or act in a certain way. You are no longer objective and you will be **fighting against what you know** for the remainder of the project.

And because of that, any user personas you create will be a lot less valuable to you than they could (or should) be.

So this is work I do at the outset of the project, before any discussions or interactions with users occur. The only things I typically know about the prospective users at this point are the following (which come from client stakeholders):

→ Their **job title** (B2B)

→ Their basic **day-to-day responsibilities** (B2B)

→ How they use the product **now**

→ What **other products** they use in conjunction

→ How the Client *thinks* they use the product

→ What **features** or functions the Client *thinks* may be important to them

These serve as draft personas whose details will be filled in once I do start having those conversations and interviews. The idea is to start unbiased and then fill in the missing pieces. Working this way also allows what you learn about emotion and situations to illuminate the facts you find later during the interview process.

What you already know will shine a light on what you hear, enabling you to clarify the connections between cause and effect.

There are two primary tools I use for this process. Both are adapted from the work of Nikki Knox, a Design & Education strategist at Cooper. She introduced empathy mapping as a simple workshop activity performed with stakeholders (or anyone responsible for product development) in order to build empathy for end users. Nikki shared her approach in an article for UX magazine titled *How to Use Persona Empathy Mapping*.

What follows are two tools that have proven to be infinitely valuable to me in terms of increasing the realism and accuracy of user motivations.

The first tool is called an **Empathy Mapping Template**. It's meant to help you establish empathy for the user and map their perceptions, pressures, influences, beliefs and goals.

The second tool is called a **Situation Mapping Template**. It's meant to help you explore all the possible situations in which the product or tool is being used, which often reveals ways in which existing or possible features become more or less useful or desirable according to what's happening at the time.

Combining both will give you a remarkably accurate sketch of a user persona whose motivations will most definitely affect your feature, function, UX and UI design decisions. These templates are available for download at ***givegoodux.com/resources***.

The Empathy Mapping Template

This template is meant to help you consider how other people think, and what they feel as a result. Its purpose is to help you take a step back from focusing on user behaviors and focus on their **emotions** and **experiences** instead. The next page shows you what this template looks like.

Start by thinking about the **sensory experiences** of the person across the six areas of the template, and write down what comes to mind as you do. Ask yourself the following questions and get down what comes to mind — remember, this is exploration, so you do **not** have to be right.

⟹ **What does s/he likely believe?** What does s/he worry about?

⟹ **Where does s/he work?** In what ways do you think that environment influences decisions or constrains the ability to act?

1

THOUGHTS & EMOTIONS:
Beliefs, convictions, motivations, worries & goals.

3

SOCIAL INFLUENCE:
Who does s/he listen to most? Friends? Bosses?
Co-workers? Outside influencers?

5

PAIN:
Fears, frustrations and perceived obstacles.

➡ **From a social perspective, who influences**

2

ENVIRONMENT:

How is s/he affected by workplace, social settings, similar products/services?

4

BEHAVIOR:

How s/he acts, and how s/he *wants* to be seen and thought of;
In the workplace and public spaces.

6

GAIN:

Wants, needs and what s/he believes constitutes success.

how s/he thinks or what s/he does – bosses or coworkers? Friends? Family?

⇒ **How does s/he want to be thought of and "seen" at work or in public?** What image is sh/e trying to project across social media?

⇒ **What fears and frustrations does s/he likely have**, and what typical obstacles to success might be present?

⇒ **What does s/he want, need or believe** to be success?

Again, these are inferred guesses, and that's OK. You will get closer to reality and throw out the things that don't apply later on in the project.

Right now the only thing that needs to happen is for you to get your brain into the purposeful habit of trying to put yourself into that person's heart and mind.

Just go – think, write and examine. You may use multiple sheets for the same person, and you may find that coming back to your work a day or two after the fact helps you see it more clearly. Don't be afraid to experiment.

The Situation Mapping Template

The situation mapping template is used to get closer to the specific situations this user might find themselves. It helps you to begin mapping connections between situational factors and needs that arise as a result.

Situational awareness, for example, is extremely important in the manufacturing industry. Workers on the shop floor now spend a significant portion of their shift working with computers — and touchscreen user interfaces — that allow them to do their jobs safely and effectively.

That means they constantly need to be aware of **what's happening** with the machine or the process, understand **what that information means to them** right now and be able to **predict what it will mean in the future**. So how they think, what they see, how they feel about it and what they do in response may determine not just their safety, but that of their co-workers too.

Situation mapping starts with describing the situation and the obstacle Jane, our user, is facing:

> *"Jane, a 911 operator, has just taken a call from a woman who is crying hysterically and possibly hyperventilating. Jane cannot understand a word the woman is saying, and the caller is not listening to the questions Jane is asking about her situation and location."*

Notice the **stress** inherent in the situation; this is important in painting a realistic picture, and helps you consider worst-case scenarios (which all design should account for).

Next, if the situation is part of a multi-step process, you describe that next step or phase. For example:

> *"The first thing Jane is required to do is ascertain the caller's location. She cannot dispatch any help to the woman until she gets this information"*

Again, note the urgency of the situation, and the obstacle Jane, our user, faces: **she cannot move to the next step in the process until something else has been done first**.

So if Jane is looking at a UI that's meant to coach her through these situations, for example, there are some immediate questions that come to mind:

⇒ What *information* does she need to access?

⇒ How *quickly* does she need to see that this information exists?

⇒ How quickly and easily does she need to be able to *access* it?

⇒ How *relevant* does that information need to be to what she's dealing with *right now* (e.g. a scripted dialogue meant to calm a caller)?

Remember that **all users operate under some level of stress**. Even if it's *good* stress, there is still a goal to accomplish, a finite amount of time to do it in and any number of potential obstacles, both large and small.

As such, whenever possible, you want to emphasize areas of stress and strain in your situations. Consider creating multiple **variations** of a situation, each with a different degree of urgency and stress. Work through each scenario, using the worksheet to guide your effort.

This makes the experience **visceral** for you and/or your team, and makes it easier to imagine how someone else might think and feel in a specific context.

Here's what the core part of the Situation Mapping Template looks like. During requirements sessions, notes and questions are captured across four categories specific to our persona:

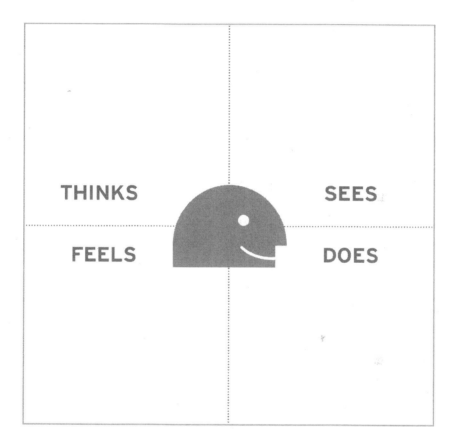

THINKS   SEES

FEELS   DOES

You're trying to put yourself in Jane's place, and the way to do that is to ask these four questions:

⇒ **What does she *think*?** What's foremost in her mind at this moment? Consider the thoughts that might be running through her mind, such as *How do I get this woman to calm down* to *I don't know what to do* to *OK Jane, stay calm.*

➡ **What does she *see*?** What information should be available to her onscreen? What might help her get control of this situation or speak to the stress she's experiencing or answer the questions she's thinking?

➡ **What does she *feel*?** What's her emotional state, and how can the system help her manage it? Again, we're designing for stress, and if Jane doesn't feel calm and in control, she'll have a hard time helping this caller.

➡ **What does she *do*?** What's the very first thing Jane needs to do or expects to be able to do? What's the first critical action she needs to take? In this scenario, Jane needs to get the woman's location, but she can't do that until she *calms the woman down*. So actions she can take toward doing that are of primary importance.

At first glance, these seem like very simple questions. But the simple act of asking them will prompt you to think through the scenario on a much deeper level.

That work, of developing empathy and establishing context, is the key to designing experiences that result in positive outcomes for all involved parties.

When You Finish: Questions to Ask

When you work through both templates you should reach a point where you've exhausted potential scenarios and have a fairly clear picture of your user persona — along with her situational and emotional motivator.

When you finish both templates, ask yourself some questions:

→ What attributes or situational factors you uncovered are **unexpected**?

→ What aspects of your persona do you think you need to **learn more** about?

→ What situation has the most **impact** on your proposed feature set?

→ What situation has the most potential to deliver **real value** to your persona?

→ What aspects of your persona or his/her situation will (or should) impact or influence your designs the *most*?

CHAPTER 8

Putting it All Together

CURRENT
LOCATION
CHANGES
ON SCREEN

} ASSUME TO
UPDATE GPS

424 clur
Peyton MD

Update GPS

OPTIONS

FIND A BAR
FIND A BEER

X

BACK Find a Bar

KEYWORD SEARCH

ALL   ▷
NEIGHBORHOOD   ▷
BEER STYLE   ▷
RECOMMENDED   17

} SAME
LIST
STYLE FOR
SECONDARY/
TERTIARY
MENUS

SEARCH

Search   (Clear All)

RATING   3 to 17 ▷
NEIGHBORHOOD   ANY   ▷
CUISINE   ANY   ▷
⌒⌒⌒   ANY   ▷
"   "   ANY   ▷
"   "   ANY   17

SEARCH

Sam   (Map All)

Displaying 6 of 6   ⓘ
Sorted by —

BAR   BEER OTHER SUC DIST
1   17   14   17   130 ▷

SORT OPTIONS

At this point, you've not only done a lot of work, you've done a lot of *thinking*. I hope it's clear by now that this thinking is the *key* to the success of anything and everything you do related to product strategy, design or development.

Think First isn't just the title of this book; it's the underlying mantra driving everything I've said thus far.

When I work with my clients' design and development teams, I tell them that what we're doing together isn't about changing the tactical work they perform on a daily basis. Instead, it's about changing the way they **think** about that work.

When you make decisions from a conscious, UX-focused perspective, the work you deliver becomes infused with that perspective. All it takes is a willingness to take sixty seconds to consider how what you're doing might affect the user's experience, for better or worse. In doing so, you'll develop a habit of filtering even the smallest decisions by asking *"how will this affect UX?"*

Before I summarize the takeaways I'd like you to remember, there's one more thing that must be said. And it's this:

> **Every single *force* that acts upon a project evolves that product's final feature set, form and function.**

Those forces may not all be obvious from the start; they rarely are. But rest assured, each and *every* decision you make will be affected by multiple factors, which are most likely (but certainly not limited to) the following:

- ➡ Audience expectations

- ➡ Client desires/fears

- ➡ Personal opinion/taste

- ➡ Cultural assumptions

- ➡ Political pressures

- ➡ Personal preferences

- ➡ Technology preferences

- ➡ Time

- ➡ Money

- ➡ Personnel

Every one of those forces has **significant impact** on whether you can or cannot include a given feature. They all have an impact on how well you will be able to define and design and develop that feature. So try not to get yourself locked into the vacuum of believing you know *exactly* what your requirements are and *exactly* how you'll design this thing.

You don't, and you shouldn't be expected to.

Yes, you've done a lot of hard work to figure out what matters, what stays and what goes. But don't believe for a *minute* that none of it will change between now and launch.

Expect that change. *Plan* on it. *Welcome* it.

Above all else, be patient, be flexible and remember that there is *always* more than one right way to do something.

Think First Takeaways

1. **Anything that was ever worth doing started with a strategy**. If you have a strategy, that means you know what you're doing, who you're doing it for and why it matters — both to you and the people you expect to use the end result. Every feature, every function, every label, every interaction and every single element that winds up in the finished product should be a direct result of these two inter-related goals.

2. **Strategy means putting people first**. Strategy means finding the sweet spots between what *users* want to make their lives easier and what the *business* needs to accomplish in order to prosper. It's about recognizing the gaps and the overlaps between those goals and thinking about how design can best serve both of these masters.

   Never forget that you always have to serve someone on the product creation side. Remember that no value coming back to the business means a failed product — or a very short-lived one.

3. **If you don't come up with a good solution to something, it's likely that you're solving the wrong problem**. The key to successful design is identifying the *right problems* to solve. Anything involving human beings is inherently messy; we can be very difficult to please, to say the very least.

So any problems related to our use of something are typically difficult.

If the problems you're examining are easy to solve, raise the red flag — because that's a sure sign you're on the *wrong path*.

4. **Innovation is a balancing act.** Innovation starts with people, with *desirability*: you may well have a great idea, but does anybody want it? In addition to what people want, you also have to determine the *feasibility* of your idea. You have to figure out whether, given your current constraints, it's possible to create something that's really high quality.

   And if that weren't enough, you also have to consider the *viability* of the product once it launches. Sustainable innovation only occurs when you're solid in *all three places* — desirability, feasibility and viability.

5. **If you fail to plan, you're planning to fail.** Clear strategy determines the strength of the customer experience. It's what informs the technology decisions we make, the features we include and the way all of it is presented and delivered. Strategic outcomes should inform how navigation, controls and content are arranged.

   When strategy isn't leveraged to determine appropriate design and functionality, the chances are very high that we've built something people don't want, won't be able to use or don't understand.

Remember, decisions that are made on the strategy plane of a UX project have a massive ripple effect all the way up the chain. So if you skimp on the strategy work or skip it altogether, you'll be paying for it repeatedly over the life of the project.

6. **There's more than one way to research.** No matter how you go about getting the information and knowledge you don't currently possess, it's research. If you are looking for clues into what needs to happen to solve a problem, guess what? You are *researching*.

    Research does not have to be a massive, academic undertaking or a formal, scientific approach to measuring variables and conducting complex experiments. You *do not* have to subscribe to, or practice, any of the number of formalized approaches to UX, design or usability research.

    The only thing you have to do is *do it*.

7. **Start with business objectives.** The core concern of any commercial entity is money. So each and every business goal relates back to either *making* money or *saving* money. So if you're serving a client (which in some cases may be yourself), your primary job as a Designer, UXer or Developer is to help these people either make money or save it.

8. **Move to users, and differentiate clearly between B2B and B2C.** You're looking to build a picture of what's going to meet their needs the best. And to

do that you need information that goes beyond how they use something. You want to know why these tasks — and completing them in a certain way — is important. You want to know what they *expect* to accomplish and why it matters to them.

Throughout the process, remain focused on the *why,* the motivation, the *desired result.* Is accomplishing Task X going to make them look good to their boss? Is accomplishing Task Y going to save them time? Is accomplishing both X and Y going to make them richer? Taller? Better looking? Whatever it is, you need to know about it.

9. **Whether you're interviewing stakeholders or users, ask open-ended questions and listen more than you talk.** Your role here is not to solve problems or suggest solutions, it's to get unbiased information. So don't give them advice, don't try to push them one way or the other. Just let them answer the question and *listen.*

    Open-ended questions often prompt silence, which allow people the necessary space to walk you through the answer.

    So be patient; let the silence following the question do the heavy lifting, and repress the urge to fill it with your own voice.

10. **You *must* ask the 3 crucial questions.** Whether you're building something from the ground up or redesigning an existing product, your marching

orders are the same: You need to find out **what's worth doing**, have a shared understanding of **what you're creating** and be absolutely sure everyone understands (and agrees on) what **value it delivers**.

11. **You *must* follow strategy with scope.** Defining scope forces everybody involved to see and address potential conflicts and rough spots, *before* time is invested in designing or building. Making sure every person has the *same understanding* of what you're building, and what it will take to do so, is critical.

    The process of defining scope ensures that you identify all those things that have the potential to derail your progress, to derail the delivered *value* of the project or the product.

12. **You *must* capture and share everything that gets agreed to.** Unless there is some common reference point that exists for everybody to refer back to as they're iterating, you will live in the land of perpetual beta. Or you will be stuck in and endless cycle of iterating and re-iterating.

    A common understanding of features, schedules, and milestones puts the end squarely in sight. It gives everybody a common reference point, a shared understanding of *what we're after* and *how we're going to get there*.

    Documentation does not (and in most cases *should* not) have to be a novel-length formal requirements or specification document. But you *must* document in some way, shape or form.

13. **Make every tradeoff strategic.** Just like many of our strategic decisions, tradeoffs are an *essential part* of scoping a product. Whether deciding what to offer or how much of it you will design or build at any given moment, you are making *tradeoffs.* You are weighing options and making choices accordingly. Be cognizant of the fact that each choice will almost always mean that you'll have to give up something else, somewhere else.

   Remember that the *balance* between what you gain and what you lose determines the *value* of what people experience.

14. **Take the time to think through and plan a "Long Wow" product evolution.** Approaching project scope from a strategic standpoint also means defining how the product will *change, evolve* and *grow* over time. It also means formulating a plan to ensure it remains relevant to people.

   Over time, as people use the product, your Long Wow should provide new experiences, recurring delight, recurring surprise and recurring *"WOW, I didn't know it could do that!"*

15. **What people *say* they need isn't the same as what they *actually* need.** And quite often, they *don't know* what they need. It's very easy for most of us to make predictions about what we would do

or how we would use something — but those predictions are usually *false*. Why? Because *imagining* how you'd use something simply isn't the same as actually using it. So remember that what you hear is really just speculation; someone is *guessing* how they would use a particular thing.

You have to dig deeper to uncover what they really need. And you also need to consider the fact that there may be some things they haven't *thought of* that might be really useful and valuable.

16. **Use scenarios are key to realistic, strategically valuable requirements.** Use scenarios enable you to generate critical requirements faster than any other process I have ever used. I've been doing this for going on three decades now, and by and large, the vast majority of what I spend my time doing is creating use scenarios.

   I've found that I get more valuable information from two hours of talking, of drawing boxes and arrows, than I've ever received from a typical eight-hour requirements session.

17. **Task completion is *not* the same as success.** The only time a tool, workflow or process is successful is when it meets all the primary *and* ancillary needs of all the people who use the product.

18. **Useful personas consider both empathetic and situational factors.** Empathy is about understanding the emotional drivers that affect a person's

behavior, because emotion will trump intellect in almost every situation users find themselves in. When you design for the emotion, you're truly designing for a *person* — instead of a collection of *possible* attributes.

Make sure you explore that person's behavioral attributes in the context of multiple situations. And remember that some level of stress is always present in *every* situation.

19. **Think first. Again and again and again. Repeatedly re-evaluate the work you're doing by putting yourself in the place of the people who will have to *use* what you create.** You have to constantly revisit all prior takeaways as the project progresses, even when you're well into coding.

As you move through planning, design, development, even testing, stop repeatedly to ask:

⇒ Does everything we're doing still serve the *value proposition* that we established?

⇒ Is it still something that's going to make people feel like it's a *worthwhile* use of their time?

⇒ Is it still easy to use?

⇒ Have we deviated anywhere?

You have to consistently and diligently go back and weigh what you're doing against all that's been uncovered, learned and discussed up to now.

The key to your success is the discipline to check, double-check and re-check, combined with a willingness to correct course when you're wrong.

20. **What's between your ears is infinitely more important than anything you can do with your hands**. The things that we all find memorable and exciting, the things we're willing to spend our time and money on, haven't really changed all that much throughout human history. The way we're wired as human beings is the key to how we perceive the things we experience.

And because of that the tactical things you do to design or build something don't matter nearly as much as what you're *thinking about* while you're doing those things. What makes you truly valuable as a UX designer or consultant is what's between your ears.

Cultivating that, learning the fundamental principles behind the things that motivate human beings, is (and will *always* be) your most important and most worthwhile endeavor.

Now It's Your Turn

Since 1989, I've helped designers, developers and project teams create better Customer and User Experiences. From strategy to features to functionality to UI design, my job is to help these organizations create differentiation and spur growth by making sure their digital products deliver the *right* experience.

I am an extremely fortunate man. The reason I've enjoyed a successful career is because, at *many* points along the way, people I looked up to and respected took time out of their very busy lives to answer an inordinate number of questions from yours truly.

At this point in my career, what matters most to me is paying that forward, sharing what works (and what doesn't) with all you brave souls out there trying to change the world.

Think First should give you a pretty clear picture of just how strategic the disciplines of User and Customer Experience are. Hopefully I've also shown you that **what you know** and **how you apply it** is infinitely more important than any formal methodology or process. Over the years I've adapted what I do, taking into account any number of established processes. I keep the parts that work, and I jettison the parts that don't.

I am ruthless about both.

All too often, the focus around User Experience Design and Customer Experience Strategy has been squarely on tactical methods and technology used. But it's the **strategic thinking** that really determines the quality and value of the interaction. It's also what makes you *valuable* to a client or an employer.

Product managers, engineers, developers and designers are all too often taught how to follow practices that are little more than paint-by-number exercises. They're taught to use technology to measure efficiency, without stopping to consider whether efficiency is *really* the problem.

Very few of us are ever explicitly taught how to create a compelling user or customer experience that delivers value to both user and creator. That's a problem, because — as most organizations have learned the hard way these last few years in particular — if you fail at the UX part, you fail. Period.

Anyone can learn to deliver great user experiences. Each and every one of you can add some measure of what I've talked about here to the work you're doing right now. All it takes is being mindful of the principles we've discussed, and allowing them to affect and inform your decisions.

Think first. Design next.

I invite you to visit my website, **givegoodux.com** and take advantage of a wealth of free tips, templates and how-to articles to help you deliver useful, valuable experiences for your customers, clients or employers.

I wish you much success on the road ahead.

See you out there.

Without Whom...

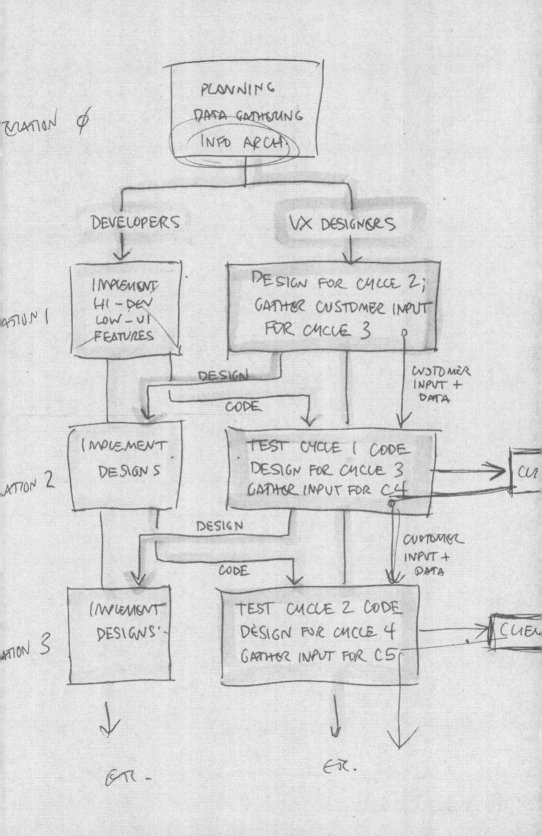

If there's any wisdom to be found between the covers of this book, it's the direct result of 26 years of relentlessly studying the work and wisdom of those who came before. Aside from the benefit of experience, so much of what I've learned has been gained from countless magazines, blog articles, seminars, books, tweets, email conversations and the like.

The principles laid out in this book, along with the sketches you see, come from more than 100 notebooks (and loose papers and the backs of business cards and napkins and...) full of notes and scribbles. I made them whenever and wherever I heard something that stopped me in my tracks and made me think *"yeah, that's it EXACTLY."* The size of my 'swipe' file, as it's called, grows exponentially every week, much to the chagrin of my wife.

I cannot possibly overestimate the value all of this captured reference information has provided to me over the last two and a half decades, and I owe a great debt to their originators I will never be able to repay.

I highly suggest you do the same. If you read something here that makes you stop and think *"YES!! That's it exactly!"* make a note. Write it down. Snap a pic with your phone. The method doesn't matter. But capture it, keep it and refer to it often.

I've always been an information sponge — I'll read anything, anywhere, anytime. I've sat in doctors offices where the only reading material was *Woman's Day* or the like — and without fail I'd pick it up and dive in. I still do that.

Insight is everywhere; all you have to do is look.

For example, how about this little thing we call the Internet? We are incredibly fortunate to live in a time where so many are willing to share their experiences so openly and honestly.

There is much to learn and again, it's safe to say that a great deal of what I practice today is born from absorbing all of this on a daily basis. From the honest admission that there will *always* be something I don't know. From a steadfast commitment to never stop learning.

When you have that stuff available in your noggin, you'll call it up and apply it when the situation arises almost unconsciously. It's kind of like finding a $20 bill in a pair of pants you haven't worn in 3 months. What an incredible, incredible gift.

So I'd be lying if I said every idea, method or process in this book is mine and mine alone. That credit must be shared with countless other UX and business professionals whose books, blogs and workshops have provided timeless principles, practices and wisdom. We are all constantly learning (and borrowing) from each other. Regardless, I strongly suggest you seek out these (and other) sources and apply the wisdom you find.

Because it's nearly impossible for me to figure out what I've learned from who from my notebooks, I thought I could at least list some of the people and sources **without whom I would never have been able to get this far**.

I owe all of them a great debt, and I will apologize now if anything I've said here is a little too close to the source for comfort.

I assure you, it's absolutely not intentional.

ARTICLES

I've mentioned a number of influential and enlightening articles throughout the book, but there are a few others I didn't reference that have been influential for me as well. Each of these, along with the overall body of work of each author, is absolutely, positively worth your time.

10 Most Common Misconceptions About User Experience Design

Whitney Hess

http://on.mash.to/1pRMv12 ▸

. . . .

What is Strategy?

Michael Porter

http://bit.ly/1HuMxol ▸

. . . .

The Long WOW

Brandon Schauer

http://bit.ly/1MrKnLm ▸

. . . .

The "What" and "Why" of Goal Pursuits: Human Needs and the Self-Determination of Behavior

Edward L. Deci and Richard M. Ryan

http://bit.ly/1CUxpTM ▸

An Atomic Theory of Fun For Game Design

Raph Koster

http://bit.ly/1DBXvFH ▸

. . . .

The Marketing Imagination

Theodore Levitt

http://bit.ly/1LBAvPk ▸

. . . .

How to Use Persona Empathy Mapping

Nikki Knox

http://bit.ly/1em3oA1 ▸

. . . .

Thirteen Tenets Of User Experience

Robert Hoekman Jr

http://bit.ly/1VFkgE0 ▸

. . . .

Rethinking Design Thinking

Dr. Don Norman

http://bit.ly/1KoyQtc ▸

BOOKS

I've read the books that follow cover to cover, and I spend a great deal of time in libraries and bookstores in a continuous effort to learn more. I take the approach that there will always be something I don't know and something I can learn from other people's experiences.

The sheer volume of brilliant writing and insight on the topics of UX, Design and business strategy is fairly staggering. But taking the time to check them out is how you expand both your understanding of both obstacles and opportunities related to good UX. Read. Often. At every possible opportunity.

The Elements of User Experience: User-Centered Design for the Web and Beyond (2nd Edition)
Jesse James Garrett
http://amzn.to/1RXFz45 ▸

. . . .

Don't Make Me Think, Revisited: A Common Sense Approach to Web Usability (3rd Edition)
Steve Krug
http://amzn.to/1HXANtC ▸

. . . .

The Design of Everyday Things: Revised and Expanded Edition
Dr. Don Norman
http://amzn.to/1RXGRMs ▸

Emotional Design: Why We Love (or Hate) Everyday Things

Dr. Don Norman

http://amzn.to/1MrH9rt ▸

. . . .

Universal Principles of Design: 125 Ways to Enhance Usability, Influence Perception, Increase Appeal, Make Better Design Decisions, and Teach through Design

William Lidwell

http://amzn.to/1RXHuWl ▸

. . . .

A Project Guide to UX Design: For User Experience Designers in the Field or in the Making (2nd Edition)

Russ Unger

http://amzn.to/1HXC4AX ▸

. . . .

About Face 3: The Essentials of Interaction Design

Alan Cooper

http://amzn.to/1RXHWEa ▸

. . . .

Intertwingled: Information Changes Everything

Peter Morville

http://amzn.to/1P4pQeq ▸

Information Architecture for the World Wide Web: Designing Large-Scale Web Sites, 3rd Edition

Peter Morville & Louis Rosenfeld

http://amzn.to/1DnHCls ▸

. . . .

Stop Pushing Me Around! A Workplace Guide for the Timid, Shy and Less Assertive

Ilise Benun

http://amzn.to/1JKm61v ▸

. . . .

The Designer's Guide To Marketing And Pricing: How To Win Clients And What To Charge Them

Ilise Benun

http://amzn.to/1P4rblm ▸

. . . .

Mobile User Experience: Patterns to Make Sense of it All

Adrian Mendoza

http://amzn.to/1CUmuct ▸

. . . .

Sketching User Experiences: Getting the Design Right and the Right Design

Bill Buxton

http://amzn.to/1HXCvv4 ▸

Design Thinking: Integrating Innovation, Customer Experience, and Brand Value

Thomas Lockwood

http://amzn.to/1TWO1hH ▸

· ·

The Ten Principles Behind Great Customer Experiences

Matt Watkinson

http://amzn.to/1TWOgtc ▸

· ·

The User Experience Team of One: A Research and Design Survival Guide

Leah Buley

http://amzn.to/1TWOnEU ▸

· ·

It's Our Research: Getting Stakeholder Buy-in for User Experience Research Projects

Tomer Sharon

http://amzn.to/1TWOws9 ▸

· ·

Interviewing Users: How to Uncover Compelling Insights

Steve Portigal

http://amzn.to/1GKo6QZ ▸

Designing Multi-Device Experiences: An Ecosystem Approach to User Experiences across Devices

Michal Levin

http://amzn.to/1SFYDiv ▸

. . . .

Designing for the Digital Age: How to Create Human-Centered Products and Services

Kim Goodwin

http://amzn.to/1SFYGuL ▸

. . . .

The UX Book: Process and Guidelines for Ensuring a Quality User Experience

Rex Hartson

http://amzn.to/1TWOTmv ▸

. . . .

Observing the User Experience, Second Edition: A Practitioner's Guide to User Research

Elizabeth Goodman

http://amzn.to/1HXDSd3 ▸

. . . .

UX for Lean Startups: Faster, Smarter User Experience Research and Design

Laura Klein

http://amzn.to/1SFYThx ▸

100 Things Every Designer Needs to Know About People

Dr. Susan Weinschenk

http://amzn.to/1Mpfmqz ▸

. . . .

100 MORE Things Every Designer Needs to Know About People

Dr. Susan Weinschenk

http://amzn.to/1Mpfo1H ▸

. . . .

The Cluetrain Manifesto: The End of Business as Usual

Rick Levine

http://amzn.to/1HXENKz ▸

. . . .

Designing Web Usability

Jakob Nielsen

http://amzn.to/1MpfNkJ ▸

. . . .

Do You Matter? How Great Design Will Make People Love Your Company

Robert Brunner

http://amzn.to/1SFZqjl ▸

. . . .

Getting Real: The Smarter, Faster, Easier Way to Build a Successful Web Application

Jason Fried

http://amzn.to/1TWPODj ▸

Rework

Jason Fried

http://amzn.to/1HXFqDW ▸

. . . .

Smashing UX Design: Foundations for Designing Online User Experiences

Jesmond Allen

http://amzn.to/1RXNkqX ▸

. . . .

The Art of the Start 2.0: The Time-Tested, Battle-Hardened Guide for Anyone Starting Anything

Guy Kawasaki

http://amzn.to/1CUpSnK ▸

. . . .

Rules For Revolutionaries: The Capitalist Manifesto for Creating and Marketing New Products and Services

Guy Kawasaki

http://amzn.to/1HNZdYy ▸

. . . .

CTOs at Work (includes an interview with yours truly ;-)

Scott E. Donaldson

http://amzn.to/1SFZYpE ▸

. . . .

Designing Business: Multiple Media, Multiple Disciplines

Clement Mok

http://amzn.to/1wjmBYX ▸

Writing and Research for Graphic Designers: A Designer's Manual to Strategic Communication and Presentation

Steven Heller

http://amzn.to/1GKtvY5 ▸

· ·

Badass: Making Users Awesome

Kathy Sierra

http://amzn.to/1LSPse8 ▸

· ·

All Marketers Are Liars: The Underground Classic That Explains How Marketing Really Works — and Why Authenticity Is the Best Marketing of All

Seth Godin

http://amzn.to/1E6sh9Y ▸

· ·

The Dip: A Little Book That Teaches You When to Quit (and When to Stick)

Seth Godin

http://amzn.to/1M3h6FF ▸

· ·

Permission Marketing: Turning Strangers into Friends and Friends into Customers

Seth Godin

http://amzn.to/1P4sr8b ▸

WEBSITES

The sheer volume of online generosity coming from UX practitioners is just incredible. Whatever you want to learn, whatever current challenge you're facing, I guarantee you can find insight and advice on any of the following sites.

The following list is composed of websites I visit on a weekly basis, with the most frequent listed first. As with books and articles, there is always something to be learned.

Give Good UX (naturally :-)

givegoodux.com ▸

. . . .

UX Magazine

uxmag.com ▸

. . . .

UX Mastery

uxmastery.com ▸

. . . .

UX Matters

uxmatters.com ▸

. . . .

UX Booth

uxbooth.com ▸

UX Movement

uxmovement.com ▸

. . . .

UX Matters

uxmatters.com ▸

. . . .

UX for the Masses

uxforthemasses.com ▸

. . . .

Putting People First (Experientia Blog)

experientia.com/blog ▸

. . . .

Boxes and Arrows

boxesandarrows.com ▸

. . . .

Fast Company: Design

fastcodesign.com ▸

. . . .

The Baymard Institute

baymard.com ▸

Luke W(roblewski)

lukew.com ▸

· ·

User Interface Engineering

uie.com ▸

· ·

Designers and Books

designersandbooks.com ▸

· ·

UXdesign.cc

uxdesign.cc ▸

· ·

Keep It Usable Blog

keepitusable.com/blog/ ▸

· ·

Smashing Magazine

smashingmagazine.com ▸

· ·

A List Apart

alistapart.com ▸

· ·

Signal vs. Noise

signalvnoise.com ▸

UXADAY

uxaday.com ▶

. . . .

52 Weeks of UX

52weeksofux.com ▶

. . . .

Nielsen Norman Group

nngroup.com/articles/ ▶

. . . .

Seth Godin's Blog

sethgodin.typepad.com ▶

> ## "I feel like I'm learning more in Joe's course than in *all 4 years* of college."

PAULO ORIONE, STUDENT

> **"Great knowledge and insight!** Joe guides you with equal parts insight and humor, exposing things you may have never thought of."
> CHITA HUNTER

> **"A Fantastic Introduction to UX.** Joe does a great job breaking each section down into easily digestible parts, coupled with real-life examples that make it easier to understand and apply."
> DUDLEY JOHN FOURNIER III

> **"Pure excellence.** I'm sharing this knowledge with my team in order to get our product to the high level of quality we've been reaching for."
> RYAN SAMSON

> **"This was a real eye-opener for me!** I found my knowledge of user experience design didn't even scratch the *surface* of what Joe covers."
> CAROL

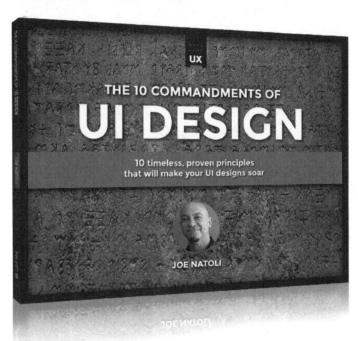

What's the best way to design a great UI? It's not what you think:

▶ It's not about having the coolest, latest technology.

▶ It's not about following the latest design trend.

▶ It's not even about colors, or graphics, or fonts.

The real secret is this: your UI design decisions have to reflect 10 timeless, proven principles that determine how people *perceive* what they see. Follow the secrets contained in the *10 Commandments of UI Design*, and you will create something that is infinitely more useful, usable and valuable.

GIVE GOOD UX
JOE NATOLI + USER EXPERIENCE CONSULTING + COACHING

TIPS & ADVICE   USER EXPERIENCE   CUSTOMER EXPERIENCE   UI DESIGN   🔍 Search

TIPS & ADVICE

How can a print designer break into UX?

This is a question I am asked several times a week, and it's a good one. It's also a hot-button item for me related to a myth I'd like to annihilate. A significant portion of the media — aided and supported by UXers in fear for their jobs — would have you believe that **UX is an exclusive club that only those with the right talent and extensive training can join.**

It's not true.

In my opinion, *every* designer — whether we're talking print design or UI design — is a UX designer to some degree. Design as a discipline starts with **visual communication**, how visual things resonate with people, and how they **interpret** and **act** on what they see. If you're a designer of any kind, you *already have* much of what you need.

I started my career in 1989 as a print designer, and all I did when I moved to UI/UX a few years later was to apply the same principles of good design that I used to design in print. We didn't even call it UX then, by the way — the term didn't exist. Many of my colleagues and I were doing the same work we have all come to know as UX. We just called it *design.*

Design is solving problems, not drawing pictures.

At Kent State University, we were taught design as a

more ▸

TIPS & ADVICE

5 Rules for Better UX Interviews

If you're responsible for helping make a product reality, then it's also your responsibility to

get UX tips, tricks, tools and insights
givegoodux.com

"passionate, engaging and *damn* insightful."

I am never anything less than honored when selected to speak at an event. It's a responsibility I take *very* seriously.

As an event planner, I know that you're placing a very large bet on my ability to engage your audience and deliver value. Your audience has taken time out of their busy lives to hear what I have to say.

So I owe it to you — and them — to deliver something that's entertaining, engaging, relevant and *applicable*. The kind of insights people can put to use the minute they get back to work.

The goals you have for your event are mine as well.

When *you* win, I do too.

I'd love to speak at your next event. Please visit my speaking page to see me in action and learn more.

givegoodux.com/speaking

reasons for abstaining from sex while she's menstruating have nothing to do with being Jewish, her ideas of cleanliness and good hygiene as well as the indirect benefits she derives from periodic abstinence are bound up in the Jewish laws of *niddah*.

In their never-ending quest to understand and define the differences between males and females, talmudic scholars spent centuries ruminating upon the implications of menstruation and childbirth. One of their more enduring conclusions was that menstruating women are impure. To avoid the taint that a menstruant puts upon anything she touches, the rabbis set up the *niddah* laws, also known as the purity laws. The crux of this legal code as it is observed today is that a woman may not have intercourse during her period (a minimum of five days). But the rabbis didn't stop there: Not only are women considered impure for the duration of menstruation, but for the seven "clean" days thereafter.

In Orthodox homes (because, lets face it, who else systematically shelves their sex life for that long?), *niddah* laws translate into roughly twelve to fourteen days of abstinence every month. Once this time is up, women cannot be considered pure until they have immersed themselves in a *mikveh*, a large tub filled at least in part with "living" water (usually rainwater or seawater). On the last night of the abstinent period, women take a regular bath or shower to ensure that they are completely clean before stepping into the *mikveh*. When they emerge, they are reborn . . . pure as rain.

Whatever the gender biases and misconceptions of the rabbis who first formulated this practice, there is no denying that *niddah* serves many vital, relationship-fortifying purposes. Even unmarried (and non-Jewish) couples have been known to reap tremendous rewards from imposing a time of separation onto their sex lives. For instance:

What do they say about you? If you need help figuring out what type of message your clothes are sending to yourself and to the world, check out the quiz in "Clothes Make the Woman" below.

• *Mind over matter:* The bar scene can bring out the worst in people. So if you're trying to stay true to yourself, you may choose to avoid it entirely for a couple of months. Use the time to pursue your interests. Take the money you would have spent and invest it in some classes. Meet new people in an environment that's caught up in mental rather than physical attributes. Or restrict your socializing to parties and dinners with friends. When you start going to bars and clubs again, you'll probably find that you no longer want to make them your main social outlet.

CLOTHES MAKE THE WOMAN

Coco Chanel once summed up exactly what's wrong with the fashion industry by saying, "I dress courtesans like chambermaids, and chambermaids like courtesans." What's so wrong with embracing who you are? For her part, Ms. Chanel never dressed like anyone other than herself. What about you? Take the following true/false quiz to find out if your wardrobe can use a little more personal flair.

1. I can go anywhere in my jeans and sneakers, even a nightclub.

2. I wouldn't be caught dead without my high heels.

3. When I go out, I dress to impress regardless of my mood or the occasion.

4. If you want to see skimpy, check out my closet. Christina Aguilera can take a page from my book.

5. When I look good, I feel good.

6. My evening clothes are 180 degrees different than my day clothes.

7. My sexiest clothes are more formfitting than revealing.

8. I'm Sporty, Posh, Baby, Ginger, and Scary all rolled up in one. When I'm feeling tough, I dress like a tomboy. When I'm feeling fun and flirty, I wear a skirt or bright colors.

9. I believe in having a few well-made, well-fitted items rather than a lot of cheap, trendy ones.

10. My clothes are way more outrageous than I am.

SCORING

Give yourself the following points for each answer and then add the points together for a total score.

1. T = 5, F = 0
2. T = 0, F = 5
3. T = 0, F = 5
4. T = 0, F = 5
5. T = 0, F = 5
6. T = 0, F = 5
7. T = 5, F = 0
8. T = 5, F = 0
9. T = 5, F = 0
10. T = 0, F = 5

RESULTS

● **40–50 = Fashion victor:** Your personality drives your choice of clothing. You don't dress to look like someone you're not or to catch men's attention. You don't have to. You know who you are and your confidence is appealing enough on its own. The only warning is that you may be a bit too comfortable. If you feel like your clothes are too conservative and don't highlight your true nature, consider investing in a few fun, new pieces.

● **25–35 = Fashion vixen:** Be careful, you're toeing a fine line. There's noth-ing wrong with wanting to get dressed up and have good time once in but you may be using your clothes and physical appearance to presen front to the world when the real one would do just as well (if not much Putting the way others see you before the way you see yourself may undermine your self-assurance in the long run.

● **0–20 = Fashion victim:** You want to look good to attract men, b don't want men who are attracted only to your looks. Unfortunately, thi actly what tends to happen when we equate sexiness with exhibitic There's a reason most guys at strip bars are more interested in the c waitresses than in the dancers: When it comes to clothing, less is not The next time you go out on the town, tone it down a few notches an what kind of reactions you encounter. They just may surprise you.

NIDDAH BREAK?

I never have sex during my period. I know a lot of women who don't care, but to me it seems unhygienic. Sometimes, it's really difficult because I've found that most guys want to have sex regardless. But I'm just not comfortable.

It's funny: I've found that my little rule often helps me dis-tinguish between guys I like and the guys I just like to have sex with. I've had a few short relationships where the sex was so good, I thought I was in love. Then my period came around and I could barely stand to be around them.

—Ellen, twenty-one, Queens, New York

Even if you're only remotely familiar with Judaic laws, you probably know that tattoos are a no-no, that cremation is you one-way ticket out of the Promised Land, and that you never ever have sex during "that time of the month." While Ellen's

- *Increased sexual appetite:* If we accept the theory that abstinence makes the heart grow fonder, sex is all the sweeter after it's been forbidden for nearly two weeks. According to most observant couples, monthly sexual separations can turn marriage into a perpetual honeymoon.

- *Increased communication: Niddah* provides couples who use sex as a primary means of connecting with an opportunity to get to know each other the old-fashioned way . . . conversation. For twelve days, couples can give their nether-regions a break and flex their spiritual and emotional muscles instead.

- *Increased harmony:* Couples who use sex to avoid facing issues that plague their marriage have no choice but to talk things through and sort out their differences. Thanks to *niddah,* relationship problems are caught before they have a chance to snowball and push the couple apart.

Although observing *niddah* is considered a mitzvah only for married couples, taking a short time-out can help you improve your relationship, appreciate sex more, take time to focus on your other interests, or just figure out how large a part sex plays in a new relationship. Best of all, since you may not be worried about answering to a "higher authority," you can choose to curtail the period of abstinence to just the days of your period and still reap the same rewards.

THE LOVE THAT DARE NOT SPEAK ITS NAME

A lot of people think it's strange that I'm a lesbian who will date only Jewish women. I don't see anything strange about it.

LILITH FAIR

I'm as much a feminist as I am a Jew. Maybe it's true that what's good for the goose is not good for the gander, but this goose wants a chance to make that decision on her own. Women deserve equal rights, equal pay, and a lot more consideration from law-making bodies. We need to be more vocal about our needs. Politically, professionally, personally, and sexually. My opinions have never been a problem with men, as far as I know. Anyone who doesn't support feminism is obviously not the right man for me.

—*Mara, twenty-six, Arlington, Virginia*

Look up the name *Lilith* in a dictionary and you'll find that it comes from a rabbinic legend about Adam's first wife who became a demon and was replaced by Eve. According to the old Hebrew tale, Eve winds up making babies and Lilith killing them. If you've never heard this story, you may wonder what Lilith did to deserve such a fate?

Unlike Eve, who was created from Adam's rib, Lilith was made from the earth like Adam. When she demanded equal rights in bed (for example, the right to be on top, to choose sexual positions, to initiate sex), Adam balked. Frustrated and at an impasse, Lilith takes the only stand she can. She turns her back on Adam and releases her sexual aggression by murdering babies. The moral of the story is that women who are aggressive and stubborn kill the male sex drive and by extension any potential children they may have. Oy.

To ask why Adam got to have a new wife while Lilith was left to take out her sexual frustration on innocent babies for the rest of her days (as opposed to, say, the other way around) is to start thinking like Mara whose quote began this section and to question centuries of Jewish tradition. The Talmud tells us that initiating sex is the dominion

of men. This in the name of sparing women the embarrassment because we Jewish ladies are far too timid to admit we want sex. Or,
rather, we'd better be if we know what's good for us. In the old days,
both making sexual demands on one's husband and speaking to him
about sex within earshot of another person were considered valid reasons for divorce without compensation.

Today, these archaic laws are obsolete, and sexually assertive
SJFs have more options. Still, the story of Lilith serves as a powerful
reminder of the patriarchal nature of Judaism and as a symbol of how
male scholars and laymen alike have traditionally demonized sexually
potent females through the ages.

*I value my Judaism. I go to a progressive congregation and study
the Torah. I want to have a family and raise my children Jewish.
To me, that means dating other Jews. At my temple, the rabbi
will officiate at gay weddings but not at interfaith weddings.*
                                    —Diana, thirty-five, Hoboken, New Jersey

Judaism and gay rights have come a long way since the days
when homosexuality was referred to as "the love that dare not
speak its name." While the Orthodox still cling to the Leviticus
decree that "man shall not lie with man as with a woman, it is
an abhorrence," (Leviticus 8:22) maintaining that the Torah is
the sacred word of God and must be followed to the letter if it is
to retain its significance, the Reform movement has encouraged
homosexuals to remain a vital part of the Jewish community by
sanctioning same-sex marriages and the ordination of gay and
lesbian clergy in 2000. Currently, the Conservative camp is de-
bating the adoption of a similar amendment. The Committee on

Jewish Law and Standards is currently reconsidering the issue. It is thought that their decision will be handed down sometime in 2004.

Nowadays, entire synagogues revolve around gay congregations. However, many Jews believe that such temples are not a sign of progress so much as a testament to the gays' and lesbians' exclusion from the mainstream community.

While the more traditional Jewish streams condemn all forms of homosexuality, they cannot point to anything in the Torah that would indicate that girl-on-girl action is verboten. In fact, from the first verse of Genesis to the last chapter of Deuteronomy, the Bible fails to include so much as a single word about lesbians.

The Talmud does address female homosexuality, but classifies it as a misdemeanor rather than the outright crime against humanity that is male homosexuality. As far back as the twelfth century, Maimonides showed tolerance for lesbian experimentation, if not lifestyle, in the *Mishneh Torah,* writing that a woman who has slept with another woman is still allowed to marry a Cohen (the holiest class of Jews). He also states that the laws of adultery do not apply to married women who transgress the wedding vows with other women. Of course, such attitudes are not surprising given what we know about prevailing male perspectives on lesbians (as in: ooooh, that's hot) versus gays (ewwww, that's not).

Through the years, the Torah's silence on the lesbian issue has trumped the Talmud's acknowledgment and led many devout Jews to conclude that lesbianism is nothing more than a figment of a warped sexual imagination. In other words, if they're not in the Torah, then lesbians don't really exist. Those traditionalists who do admit to the reality of gay women as well as men would argue that no urge is so strong that it cannot be controlled by force of will. Like the Church, they encourage the exorcism of such evil inclination through willpower and denial.

SPILLING OF THE SEED

*Most of my friends are on the pill. But I'm a smoker and worry
about breast cancer. I've also gained weight from the pill before. And the mood swings . . . forget about it. I won't do it. I
refuse to mess around with my hormones. My boyfriend hates
using condoms, so we got tested for STDs [sexually transmitted diseases] and HIV and began using the pull-out method.
He hates that too, but not as much. I don't know, sometimes
I think about going on the pill for his sake, but I know I won't.
Why can't there just be a male pill?*

— *Kim, twenty-one, Tucson, Arizona*

Even if there were a male pill, the Orthodox viewpoint would probably
denounce it as "spilling of the seed." According to talmudic scholars,
and as evidenced by the high progeny count of most Orthodox Jewish
families, a vagina is the only legitimate receptacle for semen. While
this law has only the most tenuous of ties to the Torah, the Talmud
went on to give all seed spillers a bad name.

In their infinite wisdom, and perhaps reacting to the might-makes-
right spirit of the times, Old World scholars worried that masturbation
would make women irrelevant. Women need men . . . to open jars, lift
heavy objects, connect stereo systems, and so on. But men, well, they
can pretty much fend and fight for themselves. (Evidently, soft touches,
gentle words, and tender looks weren't valued too highly back in the
day when men thanked God every day for not being born women.)

In reaction to the fear that masturbation would replace marriage
and procreation, the rabbis set up rules to guard against the solitary
vice. Here are five of the major implications:

- **Men cannot masturbate:** The first and most obvious rule against
seed spillage. Nocturnal emissions (wet dreams) are also discouraged.

To avoid such accidents, men are taught to focus on their love of God and the Torah before falling asleep.

- **Women can masturbate:** Since women have no seed to spill and there is nary a word about vibrators or self-stimulation in the Torah or Talmud, we are free to follow our urges. The sages of the talmudic era saw women as dependent on men for much more than just sex. Not foreseeing a time when men would worry about becoming obsolete, they failed to make any mention of female masturbation.

- **No unnatural sex:** Any sexual act that does not allow the sperm to fertilize the egg is considered unkosher. That means oral and anal sex are taboo . . . but only if ejaculation occurs during the act itself.

- **No prophylactics or coitus interruptus:** Again, using condoms to capture semen does not mean that the seed has not been spilled. Pulling out at the point of male orgasm is also a clear transgression. Semen → vagina. It's that simple.

- **Women can take birth control pills:** The value of human life is the only thing that trumps the command to be fruitful and multiply. If a woman's physical or mental health would be endangered by a pregnancy she is allowed to take birth control pills, use a diaphragm, and anti-spermicidal creams.

Men have been interpreting the terms in the Torah to suit their own needs for centuries. If you are not bound by the rules of religious convention and would like to do the same, focus on the emphasis that the Torah puts on protecting human life. Your life.

If premarital sex is on the agenda, be careful. Put your health above all else and use condoms to avoid AIDS and other sexually transmitted diseases. If you don't like the effect that birth control pills have on your body, by all means, don't use them. Just make sure you're protected. In Judaism, as in life, your survival is the highest priority.

To counter such logic, the gay Jewish movement has called the translation of Leviticus into question, claiming that the line denouncing homosexuality as an abhoration is far more nuanced and complex than the current thinking indicates. "The Torah doesn't include any vowels," says Diana, who is active in the gay movement. "Some of the words in phrases like 'man shall not lie with man' may have more than one meaning."

THE LAST WORD

Unlike the majority of voices in popular culture, Judaism is never flippant or cavalier about sex. Acutely aware of the force that the sex drive exerts upon each and every one of us, Jewish scholars took the whole business very seriously, going so far as to set up myriad rules and regulations to govern our sexual impulses.

Today, we are no longer bound by such strict codes of conduct. But the freedom to act any which way we please has not come without a price. For want of an externally imposed structure, we have only ourselves to rely on, only ourselves to credit, and only ourselves to blame. Whereas we once put our faith in the Torah and left it at that, we are now religious freelancers. There is no boss to crack the whip when we slack off, our well-being is related only to our self-confidence, self-discipline, and self-respect.

Just as self-help books can help us become more effective people, studying Judaism and connecting its many lessons to our own lives can enrich our understanding of our heritage and help us achieve the next level of our personal development. If you're interested in delving deeper into Judaism's views of sex, you may want to consult the books listed in Additional Resources on page 179.

Ladies and Gentiles

My relationship with my boyfriend of three years started off very casually. What began as a one-night stand turned into a three-month sexual relationship, which turned into a very serious and committed three-year relationship. Problem was he's Roman Catholic and I'm Jewish. In the beginning, I had no idea our relationship would develop into something so serious. I was just getting out of school and was more concerned about having fun and pursuing my career than anything else. We never talked about Judaism and what it meant to me—we barely even discussed marriage and family until well into our second year together.

After three years, Judaism became even more important to me. I got involved in some activist groups and started going to synagogue more. That's when I realized how important it was for me to marry a Jewish man. It wasn't fair of me to lead him

on and we broke up. He was devastated. The whole thing came
as a big shock; and a year later, he has not gotten over the
breakup. Not only do I feel guilty for leading him on, I also feel
terrible and miss him. I just wish I had realized how important
my religion was to me before getting so seriously involved in
the relationship.

—Jenna, thirty-two, Boston

No matter how many times you've heard your mother, your
nana, your rabbi, and your Jewish friends extol the virtues and
mitzvahs of marrying a fellow Jew, giving birth to little baby
Jews, and perpetuating the Chosen People, you may have found
yourself wandering off, or at least thinking about wandering off
the beaten path.

Truth be told, with all the personable and well-educated
non-Jewish boys crowding the singles market, discriminating on
the basis of religion can seem downright un-American. For all
the talk of multiculturalism, our society values homogeneity above
all else. Think back: Growing up, one of the first things we learned
about the United States is that it's a melting pot. It doesn't matter where your people came from, now that they're here, they're
just like everybody else—Americans.

Oh, if only it were so easy! As Jews, we're inclined to balk at
that kind of reasoning. Historically predisposed to stick with
our tribe, we steer clear of the strange and unfamiliar and often
segregate ourselves in the process. But considering the wealth of
great cultures this world has to offer, permanently forgoing the
possibility of learning and expanding your horizons via non-
Jews can seem as preposterous as keeping clear of Vatican City
and all its marvels for fear of seeing a crucifix.

And when all is said and done, what's the harm in dating a
shaygetz (Yiddish slang for gentile male)? It's just lunch, drinks,
maybe a dinner . . . one American breaking bread with another.

No one said anything about marriage, children, and leaving the fold.

The reality, however, is far more complex. Every relationship is a gamble. Whether the guy is Jewish or not, the risk of making a poor emotional investment hangs over the heads of every couple. And whereas an SJF may only be experimenting with non-Jewish men, once that door has been opened, the possibility of falling in love remains only too real.

Although some would insist that love conquers all, the fact of the matter is that interfaith love comes with all sorts of potentially insurmountable problems. Witness the rate of divorce for interfaith couples—a staggering 70 percent. It's like the old Yiddish proverb says: A bird and a fish can fall in love, but where will they live?

Then again, as my friend's mom was fond of telling him, "Look at me and your father . . . we fight all the time and we're both Jewish. Imagine if he wasn't even Jewish!" Clearly, a match between two Jews isn't necessarily any happier than one of the interfaith variety. The fact is that there are plenty of Jewish men and women who manage to transcend religious boundaries to forge great relationships with so-called *shiksas* and "goy boys." In fact, a great many Jews will go so far as to say that since they're not religious, they would not allow religion to become a deciding factor in their lives.

This chapter examines the following issues, issues bound to affect every Jewish woman testing the interfaith waters, whether through the most casual encounter or the most committed relationship:

- Understanding the desire to stray from the flock.

- Opening the lines of communication.

- Keeping expectations in check.

- Establishing personal/religious boundaries.

- Accepting the compromises and talking about conversion.

THE KASHRUT OF THE MATTER:
YOU AND YOU ALONE

I started seeing my first boyfriend while I was in high school. Even though my school was 75 percent Jewish, my boyfriend was Catholic. Ever since then, I've mostly dated non-Jews. Although I'd always wanted to marry someone Jewish, I would somehow wind up in long-term relationships with non-Jews. I can count the number of Jewish guys I dated on one hand, and none of those relationships lasted past three months. I'm not sure why I keep ending up with non-Jews. Maybe it's random coincidence, maybe it's that my father was too religious, or maybe it's because I didn't particularly like the Jewish kids I grew up with. Now, it's almost as if I have a bias against Jewish guys. At this rate, I'll never meet a nice, Jewish boy and I'm afraid that if I marry a non-Jew, I'll regret it and my future kids will grow up terribly confused.

—Rachel, twenty-nine, Chicago

As Jewish women, we have to examine our reasons for wanting to date non-Jews. The first step to navigating the multicultural dating waters is to assess our motivation for experimenting. All too often, we tend to act blindly, going through the motions and following our whims without really thinking about what it is that compels us to do the things we do. Ultimately, this pattern of behavior can wreak havoc on our hearts, minds, and nervous systems, propelling us into one dead-end relationship after another and wasting years of our lives. Some common reasons for drifting from the Jewish fray are the following.

- *Protracted teenage rebellion:* Not all of us SJFs are nice, Jewish girls content to do as our families would like. Some of us want to live it up and mix it up—especially if we can upset one or both of our parents in the process. Maybe we were good, obedient children in the past, and it's our time to stir up some trouble. Or maybe we just never grew out of our adolescent need to rebel. No matter when the onset of the rebellious phase, few who've experienced it can deny its general power to satisfy the passive-aggressive urges.

- *A course for adventure:* Let's face it, many of us come from areas rich in Jewish male resources. Growing up with these guys, we see them struggle with puberty, turn into adolescent jerks, and grow into nice Jewish boys. Is it any wonder that some SJFs have that "been there, done that" feeling when it comes to their male counterparts? Non-Jewish men have all the appeal of the new, the different, and the exciting.

- *Too cool for Hebrew school:* As Conservative, Reform, Reconstructionist, or secular Jews, we are most likely only somewhat religious. Even if we're Conservative and believe in the burning bush and the parting of the Red Sea, most of us are not pious observers of Kashrut (we pass on the bacon, but say "pass the lobster bisque/shrimp scampi") or the Shabbat laws (admit it, you drive on Saturdays, you big heretic you). By creating our own version of Judaism as we go along, we are often prone to bend the rules when it comes to men as well.

- *Love conquers all:* Religious or not, many of us grew up thinking we'd marry Jewish or die trying. Listening to the horror stories of our grandparents, we'd grow determined and decide to never repeat the mistakes of the past. Hearing about the sacrifices made by our great-grandparents, our hearts would swell with a burning desire to make sure their efforts were not in vain. And then, somewhere along the line, we'd stray and maybe even fall in love with a non-Jew. Now what? Facing the choice of giving up on all hope of personal happiness for some greater good or following our hearts, many of us realized that we'd choose the latter—in a heartbeat.

• *Two percent:* This lonely little number represents the Jewish population of the United States. Do the dating math, and it translates into this scary fact: Out of every fifty men you'll meet, only one may be Jewish (except, of course, in the Jewtopias of New York, Miami, LA, etc.). If you enjoy going out and meeting new people at bars and lounges, as many SJFs do, you'll have to kiss dozens of frogs before you meet your Jewish prince. Some of us don't like those odds, so we even the playing field by adopting a strict nondiscrimination policy. "I have turned down numerous men without giving them a chance simply because they are not Jewish," says Andrea, a twenty-six-year-old chef from Manhattan. "At this point I am just sick of it! I no longer want to restrict myself."

• *Fill in the blank:* You may have an entirely new and unprecedented reason for grazing in non-kosher pastures. Maybe it's a penchant for something physical, such as blond hair and blue eyes, or maybe it's that certain *je ne sais quoi*. Whatever it is, do try to get some perspective on your intentions before reading any further by taking the "Playing or Straying?" quiz below.

PLAYING OR STRAYING?

Take this quiz before you get on with the rest of this chapter. Think about the questions, consider your past behavior, and then answer as honestly and accurately as possible.

1. If your friend wants to set you up with a guy, what's the most important thing you want to know?

    a. Is he Jewish?
    b. What does he do?
    c. What does he look like?
    d. How old is he?

2. When you think of Jewish guys, your thoughts most closely resemble:

    a. You gotta love a man with a pedestal.
    b. They're all right, no different than any other guys.
    c. Are there any other kind?
    d. Zzzz . . . zzzzz . . . zzzzz . . .

3. Do you have a type? What's your type?

    a. Yes . . . tall, dark, and handsome
    b. Yes . . . Jewish
    c. Yes . . . blue eyes, light hair
    d. No

4. If you were to go on a guy-seeking vacation (translation: sex and travel), where would you be most likely to go?

    a. Italy or Spain
    b. Southern Florida or southern California
    c. Israel
    d. Someplace in Mexico or the Caribbean

5. Approximately what percentage of your past relationships have been with Jewish men?

a. 20% or less
b. 20–50%
c. 50–75%
d. 75–100%

6. What do you think of the Jewish kids you knew growing up?

a. A great group of people.
b. What a bunch of JAPs and Mama's Boys!
c. Some were okay, others not so much.
d. What Jewish kids?

7. What would your parents say if you brought home a non-Jew?

a. Thank God she found somebody!
b. Whatever makes you happy.
c. @$*#&!
d. *Moi?* Bring home a non-Jew? I don't think so.

8. Would you marry a non-Jew?

a. Sure. Bring him on.
b. I'd rather marry a Jew, but who knows? Anything is possible.
c. Only if his name was George Clooney.
d. Absolutely not, under no circumstances, never.

9. How would you characterize your family's attitude toward interfaith dating and marriage?

a. Slight disapproval
b. Tolerance
c. Open hostility
d. Encouragement

10. Why do you think you'd date a non-Jew?

   a. Usual reasons . . . smart, funny, attractive, take your pick.
   b. To try something different.
   c. Why limit myself? There's more non-Jews out there.
   d. Who said I would?

SCORING

Give yourself the following points for each answer and then add the points together for a total score.

1. a = 4, b = 3, c = 1, d = 2
2. a = 3, b = 2, c = 4, d = 1
3. a = 2, b = 4, c = 1, d = 3
4. a = 1, b = 3, c = 4, d = 2
5. a = 1, b = 2, c = 3, d = 4

6. a = 4, b = 2, c = 3, d = 1
7. a = 2, b = 1, c = 3, d = 4
8. a = 1, b = 2, c = 3, d = 4
9. a = 3, b = 2, c = 4, d = 1
10. a = 2, b = 3, c = 1, d = 4

RESULTS

● **35–40 = No cause for alarm:** You are not, will not, and never have been one to stray from the chosen flock. You tend to be conservative and follow the rules. In short, you are the reason your mother is the envy of all her friends. If you're interested in exploring some non-Jewish territory, it is probably because you want to expand your horizons. With your self-discipline, however, you'll be back in the arms of a Jewish boy in no time.

● **26–34 = On shaky ground:** There is no denying that you have a strong bond to your religious heritage. Although you're open to the many possibilities life has to offer, you value your experience and look for those who share your beliefs and your background when dating. When you do get serious with non-Jewish men, you expect them to make an effort to understand and respect your heritage. You will find a great deal of helpful advice in this chapter.

● **16–25 = Get ready for issues:** You are an individual, someone who is just as attracted to comfort and stability as to adventure and excitement. Although you have a certain affinity for and loyalty to your culture and traditions, you are also a free-thinker who is often drawn to non-Jewish men. This may cause problems down the line, so get ready to do some work as your interfaith relationships become more serious and you begin to grow more in touch with your roots.

• **10–15 = Examine your motives:** Your attitudes are far too anti-Semitic to be completely authentic. You may be reacting to a strict upbringing, bad past experiences, or cultural stereotypes. While you are not necessarily a self-hating Jew, you should seriously consider analyzing your attitudes toward your fellow Jews. But take heart . . . the fact that you're reading a book strictly for Jewish girls indicates that you may be starting down a different path.

I hope the quiz has given you some insight into your dating habits. Keep in mind that there are no right or wrong answers and no single correct way to be. All that matters is that you're happy with your general attitude.

Now is your chance to think about the reasoning behind some of your past choices and decide whether you want to continue down the same road, make some changes, or give your approach to love a complete overhaul. From here on out, this chapter will address the various issues that can arise in an SJF/SG(entile)M relationship and how to handle them to everyone's satisfaction—especially your own.

HI, MY NAME IS . . . :
THE INTRODUCTION

"Paulo . . . that was the name of the last non-Jewish guy I fell in love with. He was Italian . . . not Italian American, but fresh off Alitalia Airlines Italian. He was gorgeous. Just my type, but even better. We had great chemistry, both sexual and interpersonal.

It didn't take a lot of convincing for me to throw caution to the wind and fall in love. Of course, I'd known him only about a week, so I knew things might go wrong. What if he wasn't the person I thought he was? In the heat of the moment, that chance seemed pretty slim. In retrospect, it was anything but. I should have moved slower, paid attention to certain obvious warning signs, but I'd never been in love before. Once I had a chance to get to know him, I realized that I fell in love with an illusion—and it's not because he's not Jewish, just that he turned out to be kind of anti-Semitic. Who would have thought? In this day and age!

—Jackie, twenty-six, New York

We all know those SJFs who have the self-discipline to turn down any and all dates with non-Jews—no matter how intelligent, charming, attractive, and successful said non-Jews may be. Needless to say, if you're still reading, that's never been your problem. No, you are what's called an equal-opportunity dater.

Equal-opportunity daters fall into two categories: Those who pretty much stick with Jews until a truly outstanding specimen of the non-Jewish variety presents himself, and those who will date non-Jews just as readily as they would fellow Jews.

However different their approaches, each type of equal-opportunity dater will have to start her relationship with a non-Jew by testing his feelings and beliefs about Judaism and the Jewish people. This is where a lot of SJFs get stuck. After all, you're not going to come out and announce you're Jewish apropos of nothing. So what's a girl to do? Check out the options in "Proud to Be a Jew" on page 139.

At last . . . he knows you're Jewish, you know he's not, and you're both still raring to go. It could be just casual interest, outright lust, or something more, who knows? Anything is possible, which is exactly why it's best not to take any chances at this point.

PROUD TO BE A JEW

Don't hide your Judaism under a bushel. Here are seven great ways to let him know you're no stranger among us:

* When someone asks you about your nationality reply: "I'm German . . . German-Jewish," or "I'm a Hungarian Jew," and so forth.

* If you have even a smidgeon of pro-Israel feelings (and let's face it, what Jew doesn't?), express them.

* Tell them what you did for Hanukkah vacation ("Last Hanukkah, I went to Hawaii with my friends").

* Wear a Star of David or a chai around your neck.

* Put a mezuzah on your door.

* He says "cheers"; you say *"l'chaim"!*

* Nothing says Jewish like a *shalom* welcome mat . . . except maybe this book in your handbag.

Keep your eyes and ears alert for warning signs—just because a non-Jew wants to get to know you better doesn't necessarily mean he's the open-minded, tolerant spirit you think him to be.

GETTING TO KNOW YOU: THE FIRST FEW DATES

Once you've made it past the first few dates with your non-Jew, you may feel ready to breathe a sigh of relief. You've discussed your respective backgrounds, first memories, crazy college days,

TOP TEN SIGNS THAT AN SGM IS NOT DOWN WITH YOUR PEEPS

It's a well-known fact that ignorance and anti-Semitism go together like Sodom and Gomorrah. While we may fancy ourselves to be great at spotting and avoiding the ignoramuses and nogoodniks of this world, chew on this other well-known fact: Sexual chemistry can impair judgment faster than three rounds of Long Island Iced Tea. When you feel like you're getting swept off your feet, consult this list before going any further . . . some of the warning signs are subtle, others less so, but make no mistake, the following flags are all equally red:

- When you tell him you're Jewish, he replies: "There's a Jewish guy at my office. Mark Shapiro . . . any relation?"

- He uses the words *Jewish* and *conspiracy* in the same sentence.

- He tells you that "you don't look Jewish."

- Upon learning you're Jewish, he immediately assumes that you're loaded.

- He thinks Israel is a bad idea whose time is up, but can't say why exactly.

- He tells you that the Jews killed Jesus.

- He speaks about Jews in generalizations ("Jews are a smart group of people").

- He implies that there's a link between your thriftiness and your Judaism.

- He asks if you've ever had your nose done.

- "City folk" scare him.

hopes, dreams, most lofty ambitions, even sex . . . and he still seems perfectly normal. So far, so good.

Then again, maybe not. Frequently, with interfaith dating, the subject of religion does not come up until well into the course of the relationship. It's one of the first few things we learn on our way to young adulthood—you don't discuss politics, religion, or money in polite company. Well, polite company is one thing, and dating is quite another. Politics are important—just ask any pro-choicer who wound up dating a pro-lifer. So is money—savers and spenders are just about guaranteed to have problems down the line. Religion is no different.

- *Toot your own shofar:* Just because he knows you had a Bat Mitzvah and you know he's been baptized does not mean you've covered the religious issue in depth. The first few dates are a crucial time. Look at these as your chance not only to study the guy and put your best foot forward but to speak up about things like your religious habits, your stance on various Judaism- and faith-related issues (your belief in God, or lack thereof; your feelings about Israel; etc.), and the extent of your capacity to tolerate different cultures.

- *Listen and you shall hear:* While you're making yourself clear on the subject of religion and what it means to you, take some time to question your paramour about his feelings on, ideas about, and general knowledge of Judaism, in terms of both the people and the traditions. Also, see what you can learn about his feelings for his own religion and its place in his life. Refer to "Play 'I'll Ask the Questions'" on page 142 for some tips.

- *Make your own decision:* Asking questions and listening to the answers are all well and good, but they will prove an

PLAY "I'LL ASK THE QUESTIONS"

As you're gazing longingly into the eyes of your gentile beloved, it's important to snap out your reverie every so often to ask a few simple questions. (*Note:* To ensure that your game of "I'll Ask the Questions" does not give your inamorato third-degree burns, try to maintain a lighthearted attitude throughout—to accomplish this, strive for the tone specified below. Under no circumstances should the subject feel as if he were being tested.)

- So, am I the first Jewish girl you've ever dated? (playful, teasing, just curious, take your pick)

- Well, living in [insert name of your city here,] you must have a bunch of Jewish friends. (assuming an affirmative)

- Would you consider yourself more spiritual or religious? (keep it light . . . you're just curious)

- So if you're an agnostic/atheist, do you have trouble connecting with people who believe in God? (especially important if you believe in God)

- Being Islamic, you must have some opinion on the conflict in the Middle East? (you're curious, probing, you'd love to get a new perspective)

exercise in futility if you don't give serious weight to every answer. How do you feel about your date's ideas? Are they in line with your own thinking? Although you don't want your date to catch on to the fact that your Q&A is a test, that's exactly how you should treat it. If you find that you can't reconcile yourself to your date's opinions and habits, it's time to take matters into your own hands. Consider such an exam to be of the pass/fail variety. If the gent in question does not pass a compatibility test, give him an F and move on.

EXPECTATIONS ON THE RISE:
GETTING INVOLVED

Assuming all goes well during the initial phase of dating (your date avoids all the traps you've set, jumping through every hoop and passing every test with flying colors), you may decide to throw the proverbial yarmulke to the wind and . . . gulp, dare we even think it? . . . get involved. Well, hold it right there, SJF. Not so fast.

If there's any part of you that's still waiting for the other shoe to drop, now is not the time to ignore it. Ostensibly, you still don't know Monsieur Perfecto all that well. Okay, okay, you know the basics. If you two are still together, it's obvious that you've found someone sophisticated enough to accept all sorts of different beliefs and traditions. Despite his ancestors' penchant for celebrating Ramadan, Christmas, Kwanza, or what have you, this is someone who's been to his fair share of Bar Mitzvahs, knows enough not to wish Robbie Rosenberg a "Merry Christmas," and may even be able to spell Hanukkah . . . both ways! No doubt about it, this guy is down with our people.

Now, whether this "honorary Jew" or "Jewish by association" status is sufficient to launch your SGM into keeperville is an entirely different story. That depends solely on you and your expectations.

Steve was a bartender at a club I used to go to a lot in my last year of college. I fell in love with him right away. He wasn't Jewish, but I didn't care. He's not religious at all, so I didn't see a conflict. Our relationship started slow, but wound up lasting four years. At the end, I still loved him. I just knew that if we

THE CAPED CRUSADER

Approximately 70 percent of American men are circumcised. That's how come so many frisky women with sexual partners numbering in the double digits have yet to see their first wrapped package. Still, date non-Jews long enough and sooner or later you're likely to catch a glimpse of foreskin. Should this ever happen to you, do not be alarmed: Stop, consider your options, then vote your conscience.

• **It's a woman's right to change her mind:** If you cannot do the deed with an uncircumcised guy, feign a headache, collect your bearings, and catch the first cab out of there. Maybe you two can still be friends.

• **Look away:** Survey says that coupled with a condom, an uncut penis looks just like the regular stuff. So throw Johnny a Trojan, avert your gaze, and enjoy the ride.

• **Take, take, take:** Sure, it's nice to give oral pleasure, but if your non-Jew is uncircumcised, you may decide to keep your legendary head among your *hidden* talents.

• **Talk about it:** If you enjoy spending time with this guy too much to let a little foreskin stand in your way, you may want to discuss the issue with him . . . just wait until you're out of the bedroom to do so. Be sensitive to his feelings when you bring up the subject. Explain that being Jewish (don't say "American," unless he's foreign), you're not used to seeing the full monty and you'll need some time to get comfortable with the idea.

The truth is that with so many Americans being circumcised, your hooded gent is unlikely to be shocked by this admission and you two can have a frank discussion about unsnipped penises. Who knows, in time, you may even grow to like what the anti-circumcision crowd calls "an intact man." Consider this: In 1999, the *British Journal of Urology* published a study showing that women had more vaginal orgasms and experienced less discomfort when having sex with an uncircumcised partner.

ever decided to have kids, he would never help me to raise them Jewish. It would all be up to me, the Hebrew schools, the synagogues, everything. But who thinks about kids when they first start dating? Especially in your early twenties . . . kids are the last thing on your mind.

—Yael, twenty-six, Los Angeles

If you intend to date non-Jews, you have to figure out what you want from them. Do you want to get married? Do you want to have kids? Do you want to raise them as Jews? Do you expect your husband to help? Do you expect him to convert? These questions will have to be answered if you want to take responsibility for your choices. Going with the flow is all well and good, but when the relationship gets serious, you'll have to grab both oars and work your way through the choppy waters. To get some clarity on your goals, needs, wants, and expectations, complete the "Thinking Ahead" worksheet on page 146.

Understanding what's important to you is especially vital in the first few months of a relationship. Somewhere between one and six months into your romance, you'll probably find yourself considering a major emotional investment. The more time you spend and the more comfortable you feel with someone, the easier it is to become attached. In your initial glee, you may be tempted to forge ahead with the relationship. You may work on

THINKING AHEAD

When it comes to thinking about your future, there's no time like the present. Even if you're not seeing anyone special, it's a good idea to figure out what you want before you go about trying to get it. The following set of questions should help you formulate your views on the matter of interfaith dating and relationships.

1. Would you ever marry a non-Jew? Why or why not?

_____

_____

_____

2. What's the longest period of time you would spend in a relationship with someone you have no intention of marrying? And why?

_____

_____

_____

3. Would you marry a non-Jew if he converted?

_____

_____

_____

4. Would you ever consider converting yourself? Why or why not?

_____

_____

_____

5. Do you want to have children?

_____

_____

_____

6. If you want to have children, is it important that they be brought up in the Jewish tradition (Hebrew school, Bar/Bat Mitzvah, trip to Israel) or not?

_____

_____

_____

7. If you do want your children to grow up Jewish, do you want your husband to take an active role in your children's religious education?

_____

_____

_____

8. Would you consider merging traditions and trying to observe both your religion and that of your spouse, if it's important to him?

_____

_____

_____

9. Are there any religions you absolutely do not want in your home? If so, which ones? And why?

_____

_____

_____

10. Would you compromise any of the above for the "great love of your life" or would you sooner rethink your feelings?

_____

_____

_____

If you ever find yourself disoriented and confused, refer back to this worksheet as a guideline. Also, don't be afraid to review and edit your answers if you should ever have a change of heart.

building a foundation for deep and lasting intimacy. You may see visions of yourself and your love living happily ever after. You may want to believe that you are capable of committing to a non-Jew . . . and you may be right. But then again, you may be wrong. This is the time to stay cautious.

Deep intimacy and commitment can spell trouble for those of you who only intended to date the SGM on your road to the chuppa. Take Ari's example (okay, Ari is a guy, but his story is relevant all the same). Ari always intended to marry Jewish, but he started dating Jessica anyway, knowing full well that she wasn't Jewish. The couple celebrated three anniversaries before Ari finally worked up the resolve to break it off and signed up with JDate. That's three years of Jessica's life. Whether or not Ari was being fair to himself is one thing, we know for certain that he was not being fair to Jessica. In misleading himself, he wound up misleading a perfectly innocent party . . . and that's just bad relationship karma.

At this stage of the game, open and honest communication—both with yourself and with your SGM—is of the utmost importance. Here are some ways to keep expectations in check, whatever your situation.

ON THE ROAD TO NOWHERE

If you simply will not marry a non-Jew, you must, I repeat, you *must* tell your boyfriend. You're probably thinking easier said than done, right? Well, not necessarily. No one is saying that you should sit the guy down for a "talk" when the thought of being exclusive, much less popping the question, has yet to occur to him. Talk about your awkward moments! The last thing you want to do is to come off like a presumptuous fool, convinced that every guy is so head over heels in love, he wants you to be the mother of his children.

Insulting your SGM and making yourself look absurd are valid fears, to be sure, but they need not keep you from communicating your true intentions. There are many ways to have a "Where is this going?" discussion without sounding like you're jumping the gun. Check out "Cruel Intentions" on page 150 for ideas.

GOING PLACES

If you've asked yourself all the important questions, plumbed the depths of your soul, and come to the realization that you and your non-Jew are ready to take religion both out of the romantic equation and out of your lives, you're on the same wavelength. In other words, there's no disapproving rabbi standing between you and eternal bliss. So that just leaves the usual relationship trials and tribulations. It may last two months, two years, two decades, or a lifetime, but if and when you ever do break up, it won't be because of religious differences.

STUCK IN THE MIDDLE

Of all the places in the world, why, oh why, did you have to wind up in the middle? On the one hand, you've decided that matters of the heart know no religious boundaries. On the other, you don't want to turn your back on your roots all together. Now what?

For starters, you have to move slowly. When we meet someone we like, we tend to get a bit overzealous, thinking way too far into the future way too soon in advance. Considering the many difficulties inherent in an interfaith relationship where faith actually matters to one or both partners, it's best to test the waters before jumping into a commitment of any sort. Check out "Hold Your Horses" on page 152 for some quick tips on how to stop your expectations from taking over the country.

CRUEL INTENTIONS

Nothing takes the fun out of a great fling faster than a lovestruck Romeo (or Juliet, for that matter). The guilt, the sleepless nights, the worries of driving someone to their final exit . . . no, this simply will not do. To avoid toying with your SGM's emotions and keep from getting in over your own head, try the following tacks.

- **Predict his future—and don't be in it:** Say something along the lines of "Your next girlfriend better like PlayStation."

- **Predict your future:** "I went to a psychic today and she said I was going to marry someone Jewish. Talk about a master of the obvious!"

- **Widen the gulf:** Tell him your New Year's resolution is to start keeping kosher. Tell him you want to move to Israel and work on a kibbutz for three years. Hell, tell him you want to go back to Hebrew school and raise your children to be Orthodox . . . it doesn't matter what you tell him as long as he gets your point: Like ships that cross in the night, you two are moving in separate directions.

- **Direct hit:** Bring up the topic of religion and tell him you're dead set on marrying someone Jewish. Truth be told, honesty is the best policy.

- **Be unavailable:** Don't see him more than once a week. If he asks you why, tell him that you're not interested in becoming emotionally attached. If he asks you why again, tell him: "It's because you're not Jewish."

- **See other people:** Yes, you must continue to see other people . . . as if your life depended on it. The second you start cutting out contact with the external world in favor of your "un-boyfriend" is the second you get on the path toward inevitable heartbreak.

The next section will cover some of the challenges that an interfaith couple like you will have to deal with. When it comes to religion, there are still many questions left unanswered, so try not to make any hasty decisions before you know the full truth.

MAKING IT WORK: LONG-TERM RELATIONSHIPS

I was invited to a party by an old friend where I met my current boyfriend. He is not Jewish. We had known each other in high school and then both gone our separate ways for seven years. We had always had an attraction (Yes, he looks Jewish!) and a lot in common but when he asked me out I almost said no because of the non-Jew issue. But for lack of friends and a genuine interest in him I went and found myself having a better time with him than with any guy I dated in the past three years. Needless to say within two weeks, I was completely involved with my now-boyfriend.

I had a lot of issues with it at first, and it would stress me out to no end. But there were a lot of things that separated him (in my opinion) from the typical non-Jewish guy. He is not religious at all and has no desire to be. His parents are from South America and almost identical to Jewish parents aside from the accents. His brother, sister, and cousins are all identical to any of the Jewish kids I went to college with. His grandmother was engaged to a Jewish man after divorcing his grandfather and his sister has a Jewish boyfriend from Long Island. Ninety percent of his friends are Jewish. He was raised in the same neighborhood, schools, family environment as I was. Pretty much the only thing we don't have in common is Judaism in the religious sense. And he has already volunteered to convert if I should want him to. (I don't.) So basically what I learned from this experience is that sometimes it's more important to find

HOLD YOUR HORSES

Keeping your mind free and clear of emotional static is no small feat. Perhaps that's why so many of us make poor relationship decisions. When you're moving into an interfaith relationship, you have to stay cool, calm, and collected. Here are some quick but effective ways to get a grip on your emotional valve and make sure that cool heads prevail:

• Focus on the negative . . . no one is saying you should ignore the positive, but until you decide to pick a side (either yes, you will get invested in this relationship, or no, you will not), you might have to concentrate on your boy's drawbacks to keep from getting carried away by all the wonders his personality has to offer.

• Run cognitive interference . . . if you ever find yourself thinking months ahead and figuring your new boyfriend into the picture, stop! Remember, this may not last the week, much less the year.

• Don't use words like *love* until you've decided your relationship can stand the test of time. For now, you're interested—that's it.

• Play Diane Fossey. People are fascinating, so make like an anthropologist and study your boyfriend. When you're tired of observing the subject, experiment with him. See what he does when you show up early (for a change). See how he reacts when you don't call when you said you would. Keep a log à la *Gorillas in the Mist* and record your findings. This technique should give you some much needed distance during this tumultuous time.

someone you have a lot in common with and who loves you rather than being caught up in religion. I still don't think I could ever date someone who was non-Jewish and religious, and I

*don't think I would ever be attracted to anyone like that (which
makes it easier). I also think that if my boyfriend and I should
split I would still date only Jews. I didn't go looking for him, (I
even fought the romance aspect at the beginning) I just ended
up at the right place at the right time, and there was definite
chemistry that I didn't want to risk giving up. I don't condone
interfaith marriage and dating, but I am definitely more understanding of it and think it really depends on the person.*

—Andi, twenty-six, Miami

According to the 2001 American Jewish Identity Survey, some
52 percent of Jews are intermarrying. But we don't need a survey
to tell us the obvious. There's nary a Jew out there who doesn't
know someone either married to or seriously involved with a non-
Jew. Whatever your thoughts on this staggering stat may be, the
fact that you're still reading this chapter means that you've opened
your heart to the possibility of long-term involvement with a non-
Jew. If you should find your relationship with a gentile extending
past the six-month mark, it's time to start thinking seriously about
how you see Judaism playing into your future—if at all.

The majority of Jews are quite liberal and pluralistic. We're
open to learning about other cultures and traditions, as well as
to appropriating different aspects of those heritages into our
own lives. Some of us have New Year's trees or Hanukkah bushes
that look just like Christmas trees, we enjoy Cadbury Easter
cream eggs just as much as the next goy, and you're not the only
one who's been known to hum a Christmas carol or two when
you thought no one was listening. Going beyond the superficial,
many of our personal beliefs about turning the other cheek and
perpetuating good karma are right in step with Christianity and
Buddhism.

However, once you're in a relationship with a non-Jew, no
matter how secular or spiritual you fancy yourself, it's important

to consider what if any feelings you have toward your own people, heritage, and culture. At times, it can seem like every decision is a choice between turning your back on your birthright or turning your back on your love—but it doesn't have to be like that. Here are some ways to successfully assert your Jewishness within a long-term interfaith relationship:

EDUCATE YOURSELF

Increasing your own awareness of Jews and Judaism can be your first step toward finding the strength to stand your ground in the face of religious opposition. At this point, the opposition you'll feel will take the form of subtle pressure to scale back on your religious affiliation—and that will hold true whether your boyfriend is a Christian, a Buddhist, or an outright atheist.

No matter how far removed your ideas may be from those in the Old Testament, your Jewish identity is a matter of fact, whether or not you choose to identify with it. Before you start moving even farther away from one of the things that make you who you are, take some time to learn about Judaism and your heritage.

To keep from losing your religion within an interfaith relationship, you'll need to acquire some conviction by soaking up information about the Jewish religion, history, and culture. Hebrew school is all well and good, but all that ended years ago. How much have you done to expand your knowledge of Judaism since? Now that you're older and wiser, you can better appreciate everything those well-meaning teachers were trying so hard to instill in you. Check out the books in Additional Resources on page 179 for more information on Judaism and the Jewish people. Then, read about the problems facing Israel and Jews abroad. Go to your local Jewish outreach center and see if you can sign up for a class. Finally, consider taking a trip to Israel and learning about your heritage firsthand.

INITIATE YOUR PARTNER

Once you've begun the process of getting in touch with your Jewishness, you may find yourself wanting to talk about it to those who are close to you. Don't hold back. If Judaism is important to you, it shouldn't matter that your boyfriend isn't Jewish. Although you may feel uncomfortable when first broaching the subject, try to recognize that your apprehension is just a fear of the unknown. Once your feelings are out in the open, you'll be able to deal with whatever reaction they may elicit.

Your sudden pride in your roots can either spark your significant other's interest in Judaism or make him understand how much your heritage means to you. In either case, you can slowly start incorporating Judaism into your relationship. Invite him to your family's Passover seder, put together an impromptu Shabbat dinner, rent *Sunshine,* or take him to a lecture about the state of Israel. If he's willing to listen and makes efforts to understand, you know that you won't have to submerge your Jewish identity to maintain this relationship.

When you speak up for your values and beliefs in this manner, you're also taking the chance that your partner will be put off. As a non-Jew, he may not share your zeal for the Jewish tradition, and you can't fault him for that any more than you can fault yourself for not getting all worked up over Christianity just because you're dating Mr. Lutheran. You may hear a lot of arguments, such as:

- You're not religious, why do you care?

- Love is the most important thing, nothing else matters.

- My family is Greek Orthodox, but I'm not all "Hey, everybody! Look at me! I'm Greek Orthodox!" What's the big deal?

- Religion is a crutch. You don't need to rely on it to have an identity.

- Organized religion is so divisive. So many wars have been fought because of it. Why would you want to be a part of anything like that?

Although you should feel free to take these points into consideration, don't be afraid to stick to your guns. Armed with the necessary information, you can easily rebut each and every one of these objections. In the end, if your newfound spirituality still gives your boyfriend cause to doubt the future of your relationship, perhaps it's time to reconsider this relationship.

SET BOUNDARIES

Imagine that it's December 25 and your Catholic boyfriend invites you to midnight mass. He knows you're not religious, so his "Why not? It will be an experience" brand of reasoning is not altogether out of left field. But why is it that you feel weird about saying no and just as weird about saying yes?

Truth is, just because you're not Orthodox doesn't mean you should go along to get along. Sure, you may have gone to midnight mass before, just to check it out, see what all the hoopla is about, but now . . . well, now it's a different ball game. By saying okay within the context of a romantic relationship, you may be setting a dangerous precedent . . . and somewhere inside, you feel it.

That little Yiddish voice is trying to tell you something—namely, that you feel uncomfortable for a reason. Perhaps your partner is more spiritually bound to his belief system than you are to Judaism. Maybe you feel that you should try to be supportive. Then again, maybe you're worried that the time you spend supporting his views might be better spent trying to get in touch with your own history and spirituality. Argh! What's a kindred but independent spirit to do?!

Until you've sorted out how such concepts as religion, heritage, spirituality, and identity apply to your life, you may want to draw some hard and fast lines. Take stock of where you stand today. Account for the possibility that you may change in the future. Incorporate your partner's position into your analysis. Then sit down and discuss how far you're willing to go to support him, and how much you expect him to reciprocate. In the end, it's important that both you and your significant other walk away from the conversation with a clear understanding of each other's limitations.

JOIN THE CLUB—THE CONVERSION PROCESS

I met my husband through our work. We're both physicians, a bit on the wacky side, and as secular as can be. Before he met me, his parents wanted to send him to Lebanon to find a suitable bride. My parents just wanted me to find a nice Jewish boy. I knew that my parents would kill themselves if I married a Muslim, so I asked him to convert. If it were just me, I wouldn't have cared. But I had to do it for my family. Everyone was so thrilled to see us get married at a traditional Jewish wedding. Seeing my mother tearing up with joy was the happiest moment of my life.

—*Carrie, thirty-three, Newton, Massachussetts*

Conversion is a prickly issue for Jews. Throughout our 3,500-year history, Jews have frowned upon the idea of actively recruiting converts to the faith. Nothing has changed. That's why you won't find any Jewish missionaries proselytizing the masses. And that's why a recent American Jewish Committee study found that 70 percent of Jews do not believe that non-Jewish partners should be encouraged to convert.

Converting for the purposes of marriage is like getting married for the purposes of a green card—not kosher. According to religious authorities, conversion is authentic only if the would-be convert sincerely believes in the Torah and the Jewish value system. In other words, under no circumstances should a non-Jew ever be pressured to convert.

Since many Jews would love to see their non-Jewish partners convert to Judaism for reasons such as unity in the home, child-rearing, and family approval, it's important to discuss the subject as soon as the relationship takes a turn for the serious.

Here are some things to consider before you bring up conversion to your partner:

- Many non-Jews would not mind exploring Judaism and maybe even the possibility of converting.

- Your reasons for wanting your partner to convert.

- Your partner may be surprised by the revelation that you'd like him to convert, so give him some time to let it sink in before pursuing it further.

- How you will react if your partner refuses to consider conversion.

Once you start the dialogue, be as tactful as possible and don't exert any undue pressure on your partner. Try to be as considerate of him as he's been with you no matter what his reaction. Be honest, let him know why you wanted to talk about this, and make sure he knows that you'll understand no matter what he decides to do.

THE LAST WORD

Dating outside the faith is a controversial issue for many Jews. But with so many of us engaged in interfaith dating, ignoring the matter would be of little assistance to anyone. Since every long-term relationship begins with a single date, the goal of this chapter was to help you learn more about:

- Where you stand on the interdating issue.

- How to spot anti-Semitic beliefs in non-Jews.

- Methods of establishing spiritual and physical compatibility between you and your gentile.

- Ways to keep a relationship from going too far, too soon.

- How to assert your belief system within a romantic relationship.

If you feel the urge to learn more, see Additional Resources on page 179 for a gold mine of information about interfaith relationships.

chapter seven

Mishpoka Meshugas

"My parents are obsessed with the idea of me marrying a "nice Jewish boy." I don't ever tell them if I am dating a non-Jew. I keep it secret. And when I am dating a Jew, I often get comments such as, "well, if you guys get married." A large part of me dates Jewish men only out of respect for my parents. I personally don't feel it's all that relevant. Especially since I'm not religious in the least, and have yet to meet a Jewish guy I'd consider settling down with.

—*Robin, twenty-five, Denver*

What is there to say about Jewish parents? Parents who always put our needs above their own. Parents who go out of their way to provide us with every conceivable opportunity to succeed. Parents who only want what is best for their little girls—and who know exactly what that is even when we don't have the first clue.

Pressure, guilt, anxiety . . . you name it, we've got it. Our poor, well-intentioned parents. Sometimes it seems they can't do anything right. Whether we have the kind of mother who totes our picture around town, attempting to foist it upon any single Jewish accountant/doctor/lawyer who crosses her path, or the kind who's never met a guy worthy of so much as wining and dining her beautiful, intelligent, all-around amazing daughter, one thing is for certain: No matter what kind of parents we have, chances are we love them anyway . . . and for that we're going to have to suffer.

Not to take anything away from the emotional—and in many cases, financial—support that families provide, but the truth is that in the dating world our nearest and dearest can be just as much of a liability as an asset. They can saddle us with agendas that have nothing to do with what we want; plant seeds of doubt that may turn us against guys who inspire us with emotion; and make us feel unreasonable, selfish, and immature with just one ill-timed comment. And that's just the tip of the iceberg.

In this chapter, you'll read about the many ways that families can affect your love life, and what you can do to strike a healthy balance between familial interference and parental neglect. The following pages cover:

- The different types of Jewish parents.

- Ways of counteracting parental pressure.

- Drawing boundaries between yourself and your family.

- How our siblings can affect us, despite our best efforts not to let them.

- Listening to the sound of your internal voice.

PARENTS ARE PEOPLE TOO

*Ever since the children of my parents' friends started getting
married, they have been relentless. For the past four years, all
I've been hearing is: "Well, you're twenty-eight now. It's time
to get serious. You're twenty-nine now, shouldn't you be looking to get married. Now that you're thirty, you're not a girl anymore. You're thirty-one, when are you going to realize that life
isn't just about fun. You're thirty-two, aren't you ever going to
settle down?" The worst part is they don't care at all if I'm
happy. They just want me to get married because that's what
everyone else is doing!*

—Dana, thirty-two, New York

It's stories like Dana's that give all parents a bad name.
What separates Dana's Jewish parents from non-Jews who are
cut from a similar cloth is that Dana's parents aren't content that
she simply get married. No, they won't be satisfied until she
marries a Jew who can support her in the lifestyle to which
they've spent their whole lives getting her accustomed.

Of course, parents are humans too. As hard as it may be for
us, their children, to believe, our parents are not always right.
They are not always aware of their own intentions. And they are
not always sensitive to the effect their actions have on our psy-
ches. Then again, that's their problem. We've got our own issues
to work through.

The way we perceive and react to our parents is critical in
determining not only our relationship with them but our relationships with people who are close to us. Whether yours are the
best, most perfect parents on the face of the planet, or the worst
pair of nogoodniks to ever kiss a mezuzah, chances are they're
not that different from one of the following prototypes:

- *Mr. and Mrs. Control Freak:* "Watch your posture." "Get a haircut." "Lose some weight." "Find a husband . . . now! Now! NOW!" "No, not that guy!" Here are parents who believe that everything you do, say, and think is somehow a reflection on them. Not hip to the concept of boundaries, they don't see you as your own person and think they can control your behavior as easily as they do their own. The trouble is, they can't. And when you tell them so, you do so at risk of watching them either withdraw emotionally or cut you off financially.

- *Dr. and Mrs. Status Seeker:* These parents think they want only the best for you. They know what you *really* want. It's the same thing every SJF wants: A Jewish husband, some Jewish children, a four-bedroom, five-bath house in a nice Jewish suburb, and a Mercedes for when it's your turn to carpool. They may listen when you tell them that you'd really rather be single until you find the right person, but you can tell by the way their eyes glaze over when you speak that they're not really hearing you. They have an agenda . . . and that is to become grandparents like the rest of their circle. How much longer will they have to suffer in silence while their friends discuss wedding plans or show off pictures of their grandchildren? It just isn't fair.

- *Ma and Pa Martyr:* You know your parents love you. In fact, they never let you forget it. They call you several times a day . . . just to say, "Hey" and "Guess what? I love you." You can't really think of anything that's wrong with your parents. You guys are great friends. They're your number one fans. If anything, they're too good. They prop you up on the world's tallest pedestal, are convinced that you can do no wrong, and think that no man is worthy of your affection. Especially since your love and attention belong elsewhere—at home with them.

I'm pretty sure my parents never want to see me get married. I was living in the city for a while, but a few months ago I moved back to the suburbs to my parents' house to save some money. Now, they never want me to leave. They act like they were dead before I came back and brought them to life. It's crazy. My boyfriend is Jewish. He's also a doctor. But as far as my parents are concerned, he may as well be public enemy number one!

—Leslie, twenty-nine, Atherton, California

• *The Atypical Jews:* "You don't call. You don't write." Usually, it's our parents who tell us this. But in the case of atypical Jewish parents, we're the ones who are constantly chasing after them. Whether it's because they're divorced and have started new families, going through midlife crises, or just happy to have us out of the house so they can finally take all those cruises they've always dreamed of, they definitely didn't cry when we left for college and their interest in our lives is tepid at best. Those of us with overinvolved parents may think of these self-involved parental units as heaven on earth, but one day with the Atypicals as your mom and dad, and you'd be marrying the first guy who'd have you just to put some goddamned love in your cold life.

Control Freaks and Status Seekers differ from the Martyrs and the Atypical Jews because while the former have excessively high expectations, the latter exert a very subtle and indirect type of pressure. Since parents tend to complement one another by adopting good cop/bad cop parenting styles, chances are that each of them will fall into a different category. For instance, you may have a martyr mom and a status-seeking dad. Or you may be stuck with an atypical dad and a control freak mom. Whatever your situation, the following section should provide some tips on how to cope.

PARENTAL TREATMENT PROGRAM

Although I am sure they would love for me to date a Jewish man, I believe they are as close to "over it" as possible. This is because the guy I am living with is a complete sweetheart, and they see that he treats me well. And as they used to always say, that is what matters the most . . . how well he treats me. It also helps that he is not religious at all and does not care if our children are Jewish. And hey—they always said that that is what is most important, that my children are Jewish. So I think this is a win–win situation.

—Renata, twenty-four, Jersey City, New Jersey

We have a responsibility to our parents that goes well beyond taking care of them in their old age. By focusing our energy on creating honest bonds and true understanding, we can help them grow in ways that we as SJFs can only begin to imagine. To achieve this end goal, however, we have to forge connections that go beyond our prescribed roles of parents and children by accepting our parents as human beings first and parents second. Only when we open our eyes to who our parents really are can we expect them to do the same for us.

These seven not-so-simple steps, will have you well on your way to independence:

LET GO OF BLAME AND FORGIVE

Many of us tend to blame our parents or ourselves for past mistakes. But pain is a natural part of life. Sometimes we hurt people, and sometimes we get hurt. We don't mean to hurt anyone, just as no one means to hurt us. Still, when feelings are involved, hurt happens. When we accept that our parents are only doing the best they can with what they've got, we're much more likely to be lenient in our judgments. This newfound tolerance will give you peace of mind and allow you to move through life unburdened by the baggage of blame and guilt.

FORGET ABOUT THEIR EXPECTATIONS
AND ACCEPT YOURSELF AS YOU ARE

Living life for other people is a recipe for midlife crises. Sometimes, it can be difficult to separate our own needs from those of our parents, friends, significant others, and society in general. Other people want us to be perfect and not to have any problems because it's easier for them to accept us that way. Of course, the reality is that no one is perfect. The sooner you begin to admit that you are like everyone else, that you've got problems and issues all your own, the freer you'll be to pursue a path that makes sense to you—regardless of what the *abba* and *ema* have to say.

My last relationship broke up over an ultimatum. I know that happens all the time, but this was different. It wasn't "marry me or we're over," it was "get a graduate degree or we're through." I guess she always expected me to go back to school because her family is all doctors and lawyers. My dad is a doctor, my grandfather was a lawyer; but I love my job. I have a great career and I went to an Ivy League for undergrad. I still can't believe a graduate degree meant more to her than our relationship. When I realized how shallow and superficial she was, I knew we weren't right for each other. I hear she's now engaged to a lawyer. I wish her all the best.

—Aaron, twenty-eight, Baltimore

LISTEN TO CRITICISM AND ADVICE

Criticism and unsolicited advice drives many of us crazy. Especially when it comes from our parents. However, there is one sure-fire way to avoid feeling bad as a result of parental critiques and that is to think of criticism and advice as the critic's way of telling you about themselves. If your parents are control freaks and can't seem to notice anything but your flaws, try to sympathize with them: Either they're hard on you because they're hard on themselves, and can't accept themselves or anyone else for who they are, or they're trying to forget about their own problems by focusing on yours. Don't condemn them, feel their pain.

When a parent is giving you his or her objective advice, take it into consideration, but realize that being in the situation, you are dealing with some emotions that your well-meaning adviser is not. If your parents were in your shoes, they probably wouldn't follow their own advice either. The point is not to follow, but to hear. If you listen to the advice and notice that it makes sense, you'll feel that much closer to your parents and may even reach a new level of respect. None of which is to say that you'll actually do what they suggest. You're your own person, you'll make your own mistakes, and you'll probably learn the hard way just like they did. Then, if you ever have kids, you'll try to spare them the trouble you had to suffer—only to realize that you sound just like your mom.

GROW UP AND BE YOUR OWN PARENT

While we were growing up, our parents were responsible for us. All those years of being dependent on them financially and emotionally can make it difficult to break away. Unfortunately, the more power we give our parents the less able we are to move on with our personal growth and self-development. Slowly but surely, there comes a time when we can no longer defer to our parents' wishes and still respect ourselves in the morning. A time when we are responsible for our own actions, when we are single, childless adults and have no one to parent but ourselves. We need to strive for self-love so we can nurture ourselves and thrive emotionally as well as develop self-discipline so we motivate ourselves to achieve financially and move on to the next phase of our lives—whatever it may be.

SPEAK OUT AGAINST INJUSTICE AND STAND UP FOR YOUR RIGHTS

If your parents are overly critical and disrespectful of your boundaries, you have to let them know how they're making you feel and hold them accountable for their actions. Oftentimes, our relationships with our parents are codependent. Instead of trying to improve the situation, we contribute to the problem by maintaining the status quo because we are afraid of change. Make a commitment to change. Take some time to figure out what your parents do to disturb you and what you can do to avoid it (be that refusing to accept an allowance, moving out of their house, learning to agree to disagree, telling them that certain subjects are taboo and will result in your hanging up or leaving if broached, etc.).

My parents reacted in the complete opposite way I thought they would when G (my non-Jewish boyfriend) and I started to get serious. When we first started dating they would make little comments here and there, but as the relationship progressed and they came to know G even better (they had known him from years ago) they became 100 percent supportive of us. Now I think they like him better than me.

I always felt very pressured to date only Jews (it didn't bother me because I felt the same way), but I think because of G's reli-

gious beliefs (he has none), his family, his willingness to convert, and his general personality and background, they see that not only does he love me but we have as much in common as any Jew I could date. They feel that as long as he is willing to raise Jewish children, they are happy to see us together for a long time.

—*Andrea, twenty-seven, Dallas*

DON'T SHORTCHANGE YOUR PARENTS; TELL THE TRUTH

Lying is for children. After a certain age, we must be very careful about being honest with our parents. The more truthful we are in our interactions, the more our parents can grow to know and respect us as human beings. On the flip side, if our honesty hurts our parents' opinion of us, we need to deal with the fact that it may take them some time to accept the truth. If they take a while to come around, that is probably because they need to integrate the new information into their previous idea of who you are. In the end, though, you won't have to endure the stress and guilt of always trying to cover up the truth. And who knows? You may be surprised. If your parents think you're doing something wrong, they may actually offer some sound advice.

I have been dating my boyfriend for the past year and a half, but my parents still think I'm a virgin. They have no idea that Rob sleeps over three nights a week. And that I sleep over at his place on the other nights. If they are in the city for dinner, I always have to pretend like I'm going back to my place afterward, even though I'm actually going over to Rob's. Now Rob and I are thinking of moving in together to make things easier, but I don't know how I'm going to tell my parents. They're going to be completely shocked.

Jill, twenty-four, New York

KNOW YOURSELF, LOVE YOURSELF, FORGET YOURSELF

In that funny time between childhood and parenthood (that is, if parenthood is even on the agenda), we have a tendency to focus all our energies on ourselves. We think about how we can advance in our careers, what we need to do to become better people, and how to fix our problem areas (whether they be our thighs, our tempers, or our love lives). As a result, we tend to become very sensitive. A friend of mine told me what his father used to say, "Know yourself, love yourself, forget yourself." If we could just do that with our parents, we'd spend more time worrying about what is going on in their lives and how we can help than about what they're doing to upset, undermine, and sabotage us. Think about it: When was the last time you thought about how to cheer up one or both of your parents? Do you even know if either of them needs cheering?

WHEN GOOD SIBLINGS GO BAD

My mom would have loved for my sister or me to marry a "nice Jewish boy." Unfortunately we have both let her down there. My sister is three years older than me and was involved in the whole Jewish youth group circuit. She went on Jewish youth group retreats, had almost all Jewish friends, etc. I, on the other hand, had no Jewish friends or boyfriends. It was kind of expected that I would, more than likely, not marry a Jewish boy and she would. I think everyone was pretty secure with that (albeit, probably not overjoyed) and I was glad that my sister had covered that issue for me.

Needless to say, I was a little frazzled when she up and married a (Southern!) Catholic boy. I think for the six years be-

tween her marriage and mine, my mother harbored a fair amount of hopes that I would find myself a nice Jewish boy. At the same time, I like to think that she must have realized that was highly unlikely. Occasionally, she would try and set me up with her friends' kids, whom I usually hadn't seen since nursery school. Always managing to overlook the glaringly obvious fact that I had a boyfriend. I still tease my sister about screwing me over.

—*Randi, twenty-six, Chicago*

The relationships we have with our siblings affects all of us on a very deep level. Even if we've decided to take the "I don't care what they think" position, few people can infuriate us quite the way our brothers and sisters can . . . especially when it comes to relationship advice.

Beth, a twenty-seven-year-old SJF I interviewed, told me about her older brother, who likes to weigh in with his two cents on everything from her choice of career to her choice of boyfriend. Although Beth is not ready to settle down and has no immediate plans for marriage, her brother never misses an opportunity to point out that her current boyfriend of one year will never marry her. "I know my boyfriend, John, is commitment-phobic," Beth explained. "But I'm not looking to get married either. My life is completely up in the air right now. Still, my brother stresses me out because he's always telling me I'm wasting my time on John. He says that as a guy, he knows that by the time John is ready to settle down, I'll be past my prime and he'll find a younger woman to have kids with."

Sometimes, our siblings pressure us indirectly. Inessa, a twenty-six-year-old SJF, admitted that ever since her younger sister got engaged, she's been feeling the pressure to settle down herself. No matter what she does to try to shake the feeling, she can't seem to succeed. "Ever since my sister got married,

I've been looking at every guy as potential husband material,"
Inessa complained. "It's really annoying. I'm not having any fun
anymore."

Randi, Beth, and Inessa provide just three examples of the
many different dynamics that exist between siblings. The one
thing they all have in common is pressure. Randi feels pressure
from her mother because of her sister's actions. Beth feels pressure from her brother, who is pushing his own agenda irrespec-
tive of her wishes. And Inessa has put pressure on herself
because of her sister's marriage.

What if we all just tried to ignore the pressure? What would
happen if we suddenly saw ourselves as autonomous beings who
functioned at our own pace and did not look at life as a race,
with checkpoints to be met along the way? Is worrying about
things that are outside of our immediate control making us happier? Pressure certainly didn't make Randi trade in her gentile
boyfriend (now her husband) for a Jewish model, it didn't entice
Beth to drop her commitment-phobe in hopes of capitalizing on
what her brother calls her "prime," and it didn't inspire Inessa
to fall in love any faster.

Getting out from under the weight of other people's expectations is no doubt easier in theory than in practice, but we owe
it to ourselves to give it a shot. Try these tips whenever the world
is getting you down:

- Think about your life and make a list of everything you
  have to be thankful for (your friends, your work, your health,
  your sense of humor, your great smile, your own apart-
  ment, etc.).

- Sing a love song to yourself. Go ahead, do it. If you get
  into it and you still don't feel better, feel free to send me your
  complaints.

• Call your most supportive friend and express what's on your mind.

• Write your feelings in a journal. Take as long as you need.

• Call your brother or sister and share your frustrations. For all you know, he or she may be feeling some pressure because of you too.

LISTEN TO YOUR OWN VOICE

I moved past resenting my parents or letting them pressure me when I was in college. I think they're great. But we're pretty much as dysfunctional as they come. My dad's way of saying hi is "You're too skinny." My mom just bursts into tears. I guess this could make some people feel inadequate or guilty, but not me. I'm content with my life. It's not perfect, and it's not always happy, but overall, I think I'm doing okay.

—Lauren, twenty-four, Brooklyn, New York

The larger our families, the more voices we have around us telling us what to do, what to eat and what to think. Even if our families are small, if the personalities are large enough, their loud voices can drown out our own. Distinguishing between our own thoughts and those of our parents and siblings (sometimes even grandparents and extended families get into the act) can be a very challenging proposition when they all merge into one Greek chorus in the back of our minds.

Don't blame yourself if there are times when you feel frustrated. Sometimes you'll feel as if you're right and the family is plotting a conspiracy against you. Other times, you'll feel so wrong that you won't even be able to bring yourself to apologize. Accept this as a normal state of affairs and take steps to create some mental distance.

The process of sorting out what you believe as opposed to what your family believes begins with you. Take some time to be alone with your thoughts every day. Consider what you want out of life. Again, think about starting a journal and recording your private thoughts and feelings . . . no matter how trivial these may sometimes appear to you. Imagine what you would do if your family weren't watching. Then do it and see how it feels.

Remember, you don't have to be the best person on the face on the planet. You just have to be the best you can be at any given time. And you'll never achieve that if you're following every command but the one that's in your own heart. What fun is life, after all, if you're always trying to follow rules you had no part in setting up. Sometimes, even your own rules lose their significance. The moral of the story? Life is one long experiment. If you're doing everything "right," but you're still not happy, do something wrong and see what happens.

THE LAST WORD

The Yiddish words for family (mishpoka) and crazy (meshuga) sound a lot alike. There's good reason for this. Psychiatrists often ask people if they hear voices. When the answer is yes, antischizophrenic medication is what immediately follows. Well, for most nonschizophrenics, voices are a part of everyday life. The fact is that you'll never get away from the sound of the man and woman who gave birth to you. Hard as you try, there are certain voices that will haunt you for the rest of your livelong days. How much credence you give to these voices is what will decide whether you're a survivor of the past or its victim.

No one is saying that you should not respect your mother and your father. But ask yourself this: If you have your parents' respect, and not your own, what is your respect really worth? Give the steps in this chapter a try, then temper what you know with your parents' words of wisdom. Believe it or not, down the line, they'll probably appreciate what you have to offer that much more if you stray from the beaten path and live to tell about it.

conclusion

Last Words

"Why do Jewish women need their own dating book?" is a natural question given that the untrained eye sees an SJF as no different from a regular SWF. But there are reasons we call ourselves SJFs whether or not we ascribe to the tenets of Judaism, whereas our SWF counterparts call themselves SCF (Single Christian/Catholic Female) only if they are religious.

Our reasons are based on the fact that many of us aren't even sure how much being Jewish means to us, if anything at all . . . and yet we still restrict our dating to only 2 percent of the population. The truth is that even if we're as secular as they come, our Jewish background gives us miles of common ground when we're among fellow Jews.

I hope this book helped you explore the why's, where's and how's of dating as an SJF. Whether you arrived at some new conclusions or reaffirmed your pre-existing beliefs, you can at least say that you've given your SJF-ness some serious consideration and maybe even picked up a few tips in the process.

The foregoing pages addressed Jewish-specific dating topics, but dating is not just about being Jewish. The most popular question I heard while discussing this book with fellow SJFs was: "You're a dating expert. I need help. What's your advice?"

My advice is twofold, and while it has nothing to do with being Jewish, every SJF can profit from it:

1. GUYS ARE PEOPLE TOO.

• Strive to treat every guy you meet or go on a date with as a potential friend instead of a love interest. If the feelings develop, great; if not, you'll have a new friend or acquaintance without any unnecessary disappointment.

• Forget about the impression you're making and focus on your companion. While we women often complain about guys who go on and on about themselves, guys are perpetually surprised when women ask them questions and take a genuine interest in who they are.

2. HAVE FUN!

• If you still haven't found true love (or a husband), focus on all the wonderful things you do have. Great friends? Check. A caring family? Check. A wonderful job? Check. Great hair? Check. With all this, you're still worried about not being married? Okay, so maybe you are. We all want to fall in love with the man of our dreams—but spend no more than five minutes per day brooding on the matter. If you can't be happy with all the amazing things you've got going for you, who can?

• Enjoy every moment of your time as an SJF. This is your one opportunity to be completely selfish and explore who you are. The scary thing is, it can all be over in an instant—just one introduction and you may be saying "I do" to marriage and children and "good-bye" to unpredictability and spontanaety. Have fun while you're single . . . you have the rest of your life to be married!

The Torah takes a pretty clear position on singles. It's right there in Genesis: "It is not good for man to be alone." (Genesis 2:18) However, being single doesn't have to mean being alone. If you forge strong bonds with the people in your life and become your own best friend, you'll never be alone. In fact, that may just be what the Torah meant.

Additional Resources

CHAPTER ONE

Goldman, Ari J. *Being Jewish: The Spiritual and Cultural Practice of Judaism Today.* New York: Simon & Schuster, 2000.

Hendler, Lee Meyerhoff. *The Year Mom Got Religion: One Woman's Midlife Journey in Judaism.* Woodstock, Vermont: Jewish Lights, 1999.

Kushner, Harold S. *To Life: A Celebration of Jewish Being and Thinking.* New York, NY: Little, Brown & Company, 1993.

Robbins, Alexandra, and Abby Wilner . *The QuarterLife Crisis: The Unique Challenges of Life in Your Twenties.* Los Angeles: Tarcher, 2001.

Rushkoff, Douglas. *Nothing Sacred: The Truth About Judaism.* New York: Crown, 2003.

CHAPTER THREE

Efron, Noah. *Real Jews: Secular Versus Ultra-Orthodox: The Struggle for Jewish Identity in Israel*. New York: Basic Books, 2003.

Freedman, Samuel. *Jew vs. Jew: The Struggle for the Soul of American Jewry*. New York: Simon & Schuster, 2001.

Hirsch, Ammiel and Reinman, Yosef. *One People, Two Worlds: A Reform Rabbi and an Orthodox Rabbi Explore the Issues That Divide Them*. New York: Schocken Books, 2002.

CHAPTER FOUR

Telushkin, Joseph. *The Book of Jewish Values: A Day-by-Day Guide to Ethical Living*. New York: Bell Tower, 2000.

CHAPTER FIVE

Biale, David. *Eros and the Jews: From Biblical Israel to Contemporary America*. New York: Basic, 1992.

Boteach, Shmuley. *Kosher Sex: A Recipe for Passion and Intimacy*. New York: Doubleday, 1999.

Schneider, Susan Weidman. *Jewish and Female: Choices and Changes in Our Lives Today*. New York: Simon & Schuster, 1984.

Westheimer, Ruth K., and Mark, Jonathan. *Heavenly Sex: Sexuality in the Jewish Tradition*. New York: New York University Press, 1995.

CHAPTER SIX

Cahill, Thomas. *The Gifts of the Jews: How a Tribe of Desert Nomads Changed the Way Everyone Feels and Thinks.* New York: Doubleday, 1998.

Crohn, Joel. *Mixed Matches : How to Create Successful Interracial, Interethnic, and Interfaith Relationships.* Greenwhich, CT: Fawcett, 1995.

Dimont, Max I. *Jews, God, and History.* New York: Simon & Schuster, 1962.

Hawxhurst, Joan C. *Interfaith Family Guidebook: Practical Advice for Jewish and Christian Partners.* Kalamazoo, MI: Dovetail, 1998.

Johnson, Paul. *A History of the Jews.* New York: HarperCollins, 1988.

Kolatch, Alfred J. *The Jewish Book of Why.* New York: Jonathan David, 1981.

Richardson, Brenda Lane. *Guess Who's Coming to Dinner: Celebrating Interethnic, Interfaith, and Interracial Relationships.* Berkeley: Wildcat Canyon Press, 2000.

Rosenbaum, Mary Helene, and Stanley Rosenbaum. *Celebrating Our Differences.* Shippensburg, PA: Ragged Edge Press, 2001.

Rozakis, Laurie E. *The Complete Idiot's Guide to Interfaith Relationships.* New York: Alpha, 2001.

Telushkin, Joseph. *Jewish Literacy: The Most Important Things to Know about the Jewish Religion, Its People and Its History.* New York: William Morrow, 1991.

index

about the author

Leah Furman is an SJF living in New York City. Ever since she wrote *The Everything after College Book,* a survival guide for recent college graduates, she has been writing on subjects ranging from dating to celebrities. As a dating expert, she has given seminars, appeared on numerous television and radio shows, and is frequently quoted in publications such as *Cosmopolitan.* To read more about being an SJF or to contact Leah, go to www.leahfurman.com.